DUNNY MAN'S PICNIC

DUNNY MAN'S PICNIC

A War Bride's Journey

Diana Marie Fodero

iUniverse, Inc.
New York Bloomington

DUNNY MAN'S PICNIC

A War Bride's Journey

iUniverse books may be ordered through booksellers or by contacting:

iUniverse
1663 Liberty Drive
Bloomington, IN 47403
www.iuniverse.com
1-800-Authors (1-800-288-4677)

ISBN: 978-0-595-48287-0 (pbk)
ISBN: 978-0-595-49385-2(cloth)
ISBN: 978-0-595-60374-9 (ebk)

Printed in the United States of America

TO GLADYS

Contents

Foreword

I started to write this story for my two daughters and their children, thinking that one day they might want to know more of their mother and grandmother's life. It started out as a rather ordinary story of struggles and hardships that many women face, both then and now. It was intended to be read by them alone. To my joyful and sometimes difficult surprise, it turned out to be a journey for myself, answering questions that had been buried in my soul, mired down by the dread of vulnerable exposure.

Details and sharpness of memory evolved, presented to me as a gift, as if I were that child back in that little flat in Redfern, hearing about my mother's life in America. I began remembering words, moods, and even facial expressions, travelling on to my own early years with remarkable detail. What I once thought of as a fractured family became defined by lessons learned from the strengths of the human spirit. Secrets that we keep from our past, the burden of the sins of our fathers, can only be put to rest, where it truly belongs, when honestly confronted with raw truth. Only then can we open the curtain and fling the lurking parasites into oblivion. I was blessed to have the support of my husband, Greg, through this, holding my hand with the wisdom of knowing when the right moments were to squeeze my fingers and to allow me my tears.

I have a quilt hanging on my wall, a gift from a friend who refused to use the ordinary patterns, suggested fabric, and guidelines set forth by the rules of her quilting guild. She made it from scraps picked up from the floor, discarded rich pieces of gold silk, bronze taffeta and burgundy brocade. All shapes and sizes were woven tightly together to make a treasured crazy quilt. In the end it all came together as one unique piece of art, as individual as each of our God-given lives that belong to us alone.

1

NO YANKS

When my grandfather George got the sack from the Australian Post Master General's Office on that April day in 1939, it was "some bloody pommy's fault". He had been delivering mail for the past twenty years, starting his days sharply at 8 AM, when he climbed up the rickety steps and weaved his way up the gradual rise of the cobbled street along the rocky ridges of the area next to the west side of Sydney Harbour. Never becoming bored or tired of this route or his daily tasks my grandfather embraced each day with renewed enthusiasm. Looking down from the hill he could see the familiar green and yellow ferries scurrying and darting like worker bees, beginning their day, just like him, both dwarfed on some mornings by the Queen Bee of the harbour, a large ocean liner that had arrived from far-away ports the night before. His duty was to deliver mail to each small shanty house, five pubs and boarding houses intertwined with several refined terrace houses—the area that had been planned on paper years before by the city's visionaries. Execution of those visions would be completed by the sweat and back-breaking labour of men who were convicted of crimes in a hemisphere far from these shores where they would inevitably die, homesick and physically broken. The imposing new bridge, completed several years before, had been a wonder to George, and he had followed its slow progress each day, sitting on the shoreline after his mailbag was emptied. It finally came together when the two spans met in the middle with wondered engineering precision. Every night when he returned home he would stop by his friend Pat's pub and tell him of the progress of the Sydney Harbour Bridge. It pleased him that that his uniform sometimes seemed to be the same colour of the rocks and stones that made up this small neighbourhood. Refusing to change to a summer uniform, he preferred the bluish-grey shade of the heavy serge material that made up his winter pants and jacket. Strangely, it gave him a feeling that he was as permanent as the earth beneath his feet and would always be so.

Building of the Sydney Harbour Bridge, completed in 1932

After returning from a war that had cruelly plucked sixty thousand Australian lives out of the country's population of five million, his gratitude for being one of the lucky ones to return alive to the country of his birth was mixed with confusion and guilt. To believe it was the same kind God of his youth that spared his ordinary life invited so many doubts and questions. Why him, and why not them? He would struggle for many years with that question. How could he honour a selective God, one who stood by like a Nazi soldier pointing to who goes to the work camp and, with a casual hand motion, determined those whose destiny was the gas chamber. During his lifetime that question would never be answered, and it didn't need to be, once he truly believed that the kind God of his young life had vanished, gone the way of Father Christmas and all his childhood myths.

He had vowed many years before as a young man to embrace the mundane routine, grateful for a chance to return from France to his home with only mental scars of his journey. He would live a simple life when he returned from war, he thought. Forget about all the blood and hunger. "What's in the past is over," his logical self would constantly mumble, shaking his head, trying to fling away the vision of these young, desperate faces that refused to be flung. When he first returned from his war, they were occasional unwelcome visitors he could shoo away, quickly replaced by the distractions of youth. Time was not erasing them, they hadn't moved on, and he had to give up, as they were getting stronger and refused to be banished from his mind. These young dying faces were always there with him now, and he lived with their despair.

It was a typical Sydney autumn day back in 1939 with it's damp cool morning, but after 10:00 AM the beating sun on the stone streets made the weight of the bag pulling on his small frame feel like he was carrying a heavy boulder, just like the ones that made up the foundations of the area's cottages and pubs.

At every pub some "good-hearted bugga" would shout him a beer. "Give the little digger a schooner," they would say to the publican. "It was a pommy who dobbed him in," my mother told me every ANZAC Day, when, after a few glasses of plonk, this story was oddly patriotic and strangely meant to honour his memory.

"He was just sittin' in the gutter, takin' a rest from the heat, just gettin' his letters lined up and pullin' himself together, countin' how many letters he had to go, when a gust of wind came up and blew all the bloody letters down Argyle Street. Some bloody pommy sticky beak livin' across the street rode his bike down to Martin Place and spoke to the PMG supervisor, told him the little mailman that delivers the letters every day had been in the Lord Nelson for over an hour, came out, sat in the gutter, fell asleep, and the mail was blowin' all over the street." She said the charge of answering this complaint was given to a young worker, a supervisor in training—a scared young man, she said, who heard about the area near the bridge, the daily fights, and the wharfies who worked down on the loading docks, whose social introduction to each other was a punch, not a handshake. He dreaded the walk up the hill next to the quay, where the smell of steam from the passenger ferries mingled with fried onions and eggs from the hamburger cafés. He passed the women sitting on the steps of the terrace houses, their hair set in bobby pins, an act of hope for a night of romance, perhaps dance tonight, and not suffer the usual neglect or a smack from a drunken husband.

Every few steps he would bend over, shaking his head, and stoop to pick up undelivered letters and pension checks postmarked from all over Australia and beyond. Some overseas letters had landed in the gutter, one in the middle of the road, and two pension checks caught between the thorny branches of a shrub in front of a neat brick terrace house. Always suspicious of a man dressed in a suit, the "lady of the house", while polishing the brass door-knocker, was aware of his every move and had watched him approach. When he reached for the thorn-captured mail, she grabbed her broom and hit him over the head, then shoved the bristles in the poor fellow's mouth, pushing him to the edge of the gutter and into the street. "Don't come up here sticky beakin' around, you bloody bludger."

Grabbing the mail, he walked briskly towards the Lord Nelson, anxious to get this errand over, and found George lying asleep in the gutter. When the street and the pub were quiet without the expected raucous patrons, it seemed rather dignified with English charm. He would try to pick him up, take George back to the office, give him a cup of tea, let him sober up, and then maybe the head supervisor could give him "a good talking to". When he got him halfway to his feet, his benevolent feeling of tolerance and charity dissipated, and he lost the fight to the smell of urine and the sight of my grandfather's wet pants. As the years went on new characters appeared in this story; their thoughts had clarity depending on how much plonk my mother had to drink. Some years two blokes chased the young man down the street, and some years they stayed put at the pub's massive portals. Two sweaty men with red faces, purple veins running through their sunburned noses, dressed in blue singlets would shout orders from the pub door, all the while hanging on to a schooner of Tooheys, "Leave the poor bugga alone, you bloody mug."

When they were joined at the door by four more sweaty faces enticed out of the building by a hint of a good fight, the young man shook his head. "I give up," he said, gently dropping smelly George back in the gutter. He turned and walked away, glancing back every few steps to make sure no one was on his heels. Instead, they were dragging my inebriated grandfather into the pub, his bodily functions staining the footpath in front of the Lord Nelson Hotel. Hoping this would be the last time he would ever have reason to walk up to these slums again, the young man in charge of employee complaints stated in his daily report that he had found Mr. Yeats drunk, slovenly, and not a fit representative of the Australian Post Master General's Office. A letter went out that afternoon advising that the little digger's service would no longer be required.

The Lord Nelson Hotel

On ANZAC Day, Australians honour the brave young men from Australia and New Zealand who battled unbeatable odds with courage and humour, along with those slaughtered by the careless miscalculation of the British military establishment in Gallipoli. My ANZAC Day story, however, was not about this lesson in history; the story told to me every ANZAC Day was how my grandfather pissed his pants in the gutter in front of the Lord Nelson Hotel and lost his job due to some Englishman who had the ridiculous notion that people deserved to get their mail. After a few years, I grew tired of the story and would question the changing facts and vivid detail. I would not learn until many years later the futility of the search for provable truth from this woman with an inherent Irish imagination inflamed by cheap Aussie wine. I would ask my mother how she knew that the bloke that dobbed him in was a pommy.

"It wasn't Australian to complain, even about lost letters, especially some poor old ANZAC. You'd never have a day's luck if you did that." No, she knew it was definitely a pommy.

As the story went … well, at least some years it went this way.

The two big wharfies dragged George back into the pub, laid him across a bench where he slept until the pub was closing at six o'clock, and then they carried him down to the tram stop in front of the Ship Inn Hotel at Circular Quay. They laid him across the slatted wooden seats on the Rosebery tram. "There ya go, mate."

Lullabied back to sleep by the familiar clank of steel against steel, he passed his stop in Zetland and would ride on to Rosebery to the end of the route and back. At the time Zetland was a working-class area of mostly freestanding homes, factories, and stables, sometimes referred to as Irish Town and a mere five kilometres from the city.

My mother's best friend, Gladys, lived right in front of the tram stop. If she was outside, she would watch him walk over to the pub, knowing that my mother might call upon her later to help take him home. She would wave to her friend's father and if she was inside, she would still watch his journey across the road, peeking behind the lace curtains of the parlour. Gladys naturally shared her friend's burdens, especially the role of caretaker, a role she had slid into silently sometime during their childhood. Peggy and Gladys had gone to school together since they were in kindergarten. My mother left school at age fourteen because Sister Ann said she was wasting both of their time. "Better learn a trade, my girl, as no boy from a good Catholic family will marry a cheeky girl like you, swearing and not the least bit interested in housekeeping." With practical common sense and full understanding of the limited choices available, Sister Ann called the printing factory nearby, using her religious clout with the manager, a good Catholic man who would rather die than refuse a nun any favour. My mother started working the next day, promising this wise old nun that she would learn a trade and say a Hail Mary every day, a promise she kept until her death.

Gladys and Peggy, age nineteen. Taken at Martin Place, Sydney, 1938

That night, the eve of ANZAC Day, Gladys ran over to my mother's house dodging cars and horses. "Peggy, I saw your father whizzin' by in the tram. I couldn't catch it in time to hop on and get him off; he's probably on the way to whoop-whoop by now."

"Alright, Glad, we'll wait for the tram to turn around, jump on, grab an arm each, and drag him off."

When the tram turned the corner on it's way back to the city, they both hopped on, grabbing George under each arm. With his feet dangling six inches off the floor, they lifted him up, out of the tram, and onto the footpath.

"Tomorrow's ANZAC Day, Dadda, you have to be up bright and early."

"Yes, luv, I'll see me old mate Mick, and we'll have a good old gay and hearty."

When they walked into their small house, George's dinner was balancing on the lid of the garbage can.

"Where's Dadda's tea, Mumma?"

"Dinner is at five o'clock, not eight," she said lifting the lid of the garbage can, exposing the cold dinner.

"That's alright, luv, I'll go to bed. Feel a bit crook anyway, will see me mate Mick tomorrow."

"And don't be bringing Mick back here after the march. I don't want the two of you sitting in the backyard drinking and singing *Danny Boy* over and over, embarrassing me in front of the neighbours," my grandmother said

It had been a good day, he thought with everyone shouting him a drink at each pub. He sat down unsteadily on the edge of the wooden double bed he shared with Maude. He smiled down at his beautiful daughter as she untied his shoes and handed him his neatly folded pyjamas.

On most nights he got off the tram at five o'clock sharp and went in to the corner pub that belonged to his friend Pat. Except for the hour between five and six George was easy going and slow moving. Between five and six o'clock in Australian pubs, men became guzzling, swilling monsters in a frenzy to drink as much as they could, fighting for a place at the bar before the pubs were required by law to close at six o'clock. "Not bloody fair to the working man," they complained.

Although on Sunday the pub was closed and routinely hosed down with Lysol, Pat would leave the last door at the end open, hoping his friend would spend an hour with him while all the women were at nine o'clock Mass. He would wave his little mate to come in and pour a cup of tea. Never willing to break the law and serve beer on Sundays, he wouldn't even step behind the bar. He stuck to the rules, no drinking on Sunday. He wasn't going to lose his pub; it was the only job he knew. Whenever he could, after hosing down the pub, Pat read the Sydney papers, the London papers, and the *New York Times*, sent from his daughter in London and friends in New York. "Listen to this," he would say to anyone who would listen or feign the slightest interest. The foreign news was always at least three months old, the length of time it took for boat mail to arrive from England or New York.

"Did you hear what that mug Menzies said the other day?" The sentence was the same throughout the years, only the names changed, from Cook up to Menzies. The current prime minister was always a "mug". On those peaceful Sundays with Pat, George would talk about the battles in France and his years in the war. Pat always talked about a special day in 1917, while George was off in France. As a member of the Catholic Guild he had helped at the funeral viewing of the Australian boxing legend Les Darcy, when his body came home from a boxing match in America. "Aw, mate, you should've seen it … hundreds of people, paying their respects." Always wary of America and Americans except for only one, they both believed that the Australian boxer had died suspiciously in Memphis, possibly murdered by his American competitors. The one and only American that they liked was Will Rogers. They read every column he wrote and saved their favourites quotes in a leather-bound book and simply called it "Will's Words".

"Listen to this, George: *The best way to make fire with two sticks is to make sure one of them is a match*."

They laughed and shook their head as they had many times before, same quotes, different day.

Will Rogers visits Australia with the Wirth Circus

As young boys George and Pat saw the American cowboy Will Rogers when he toured Australia with the Wirth Circus and since that time had claimed him as their friend. Reasons for their alliance to this folksy American humorist were different for each man. George felt connected to Rogers by his physical appearance, as they both shared the same height and shy looks; Pat felt connected by a witty level of intellect. Over the years the two followed the cowboy's career with proprietary approval. This beloved American Indian, so far away from Australia, maturing from cattle-roping tricks to the eventual observations of war and politics, gave both of these men a shared perception of the world around them, gift wrapped in words just for them:

Live in such a way that you would not be ashamed to sell your parrot to the town
gossip.
An onion can make people cry but no vegetable can make people laugh.
People don't change under governments; governments change, people remain the same.
Good judgment comes from experience, and a lot of that comes from bad judgment.

Pat inherited the legacy of pub ownership from his father, and the only thing he could remember about big Pat Sullivan was that he was always sweating and breaking up fights. At age sixteen young Pat lost his right arm while working at the brickworks when a buckboard carrying bricks overturned, pinning him under the wheel and shattering his arm from the elbow down to his fingers. Those few minutes changed his life and destiny; he would carry on his father's legacy, his lifelong dream as a rugby fullback switched off in that painful second. With one good arm, he could wipe down the bar, wash the glasses, pour a schooner, and jab the back of some loudmouth troublemaker. The left arm grew incredibly strong, and he could kick two people out of the pub while his left arm jabbed at their back, forcing their breath out two feet ahead of their bodies.

As the years went by, Pat lost interest in trying to top George's stories of France during the war and the willing French girls, which he suspected was bullshit anyway. He did not care that the Yanks were coming into this new bloody war; he did not care about the prime minister or even if Australia was taken over by the "bloody Japs". He still kept the one door open for George every Sunday, but they mostly sat in silence, unread newspapers stacked in a corner. Two men who talked nonstop every Sunday for years, bonded by humour and a cowboy philosopher, did not know what to say after Pat's only son, Michael, was found dead in the park, hanging from a tree. Rumours spread that Michael was a "poofta" after Michael's girlfriend, Jean, told her brothers that Michael never got a "hardie" with her. She had caught Michael and the new Australian bloke who worked at the butcher shop hugging each other. The butcher was patting Michael on the bum.

George knew that anything he could say to his friend to cheer him up would be useless, so they would sit together. Occasionally, they would glance up at the picture on the wall of a young, bright-eyed boxer, poised in his boxing gloves, ready to take on the world; who had come home in a coffin at the young age of twenty one. Then they would look down to the stack of yellowing newspaper clippings in the corner. Will Rogers was killed in a plane crash in 1935, and they felt the loss personally, as if their favourite brother had abandoned them. Again they sat in silence, not able to give or take comfort in words anymore but only in each other's silent, fragile presence.

George and Maude Yeats adopted Margaret Dorothy Kennedy, my mother, when she was an infant. They called her Peggy, changed her last name to Yeats, and forgot that she was adopted, except when they had a reason to reach in the back of their bedroom wardrobe and would feel the tin can that contained the official adoption papers.

When Peggy "played up," Maude said she took after her father, George, while people looked at her quizzically and told their children, "Don't go too close to her; her real mother is in the nut house" and "What's in the blood has a way of coming out. You mark my words—sooner or later it will come out and that girl will end up no good."

With the help of her daughter, Maude had tea ready every night at five o'clock sharp, despite her daughter's arguments.

"Mumma, you know Dadda's not going to get home till after the pub closes, and even then Pat has to wait to clean up and close the pub to help him up the back lane."

"If he came straight home from work, he would have time to wash up and have dinner at five."

"But his dinner is always dried up; the meat is like bloody shoe leather."

"Don't swear at me, young lady," Maude would say. "You always stick up for him. He's a no-hoper drunk, and I am not going to cook after the pub's closing time … and that's not the way you peel potatoes. How many times have I told you not to take so much of the potato with the skin? Waste not, want not."

"Doesn't seem to make any difference," Peggy would allow. "We're still wantin'."

No words would be spoken between the two women for the rest of the night.

Every weeknight around quarter past six, Peggy would go into the backyard and look over the fence and down the lane for Pat, who would be dragging home the drunken father she adored. As soon as they turned the corner she would open the gate and walk down to meet them, saying "Hello, Dadda". She'd smile gratefully at Pat, who would release his arm from under George and hand him over to his daughter, a move they had perfected with the practiced grace of smoothly changing partners in a two-step, the moves that caretakers of a drunk know all too well: your right arm under the left and around their back.

"Gotta go to the loo, luv," George would say.

Peggy would gently loosen his pants and then place him on the wooden bench over the hole in the backyard dunny. After twenty minutes in the kitchen, unable to bear her mother's cold silence any longer, Peggy would walk down the narrow backyard.

"You alright, Dadda? Come on and have your tea."

He was usually asleep and the dinner dried up and cold: boiled meat, boiled potatoes, and sometimes boiled pumpkin or wrinkled peas.

"Have a cuppa, Dadda, and then off to bed."

"Alright, luv, you're a good girl. Watch out for these bludgers around here. They'll promise you the moon and give you dirt."

As the years went by, George added a sentence to his nightly speech, now that they were in the middle of another war. "Those bloody Yanks are in Sydney now, luv. Cocky buggas. You stay away from them, don't trust em—you know what happened to poor old Les Darcy ... *Oh, Danny boy, the pipes the pipes are calling ...*"

"No, Dadda, I promise no Yanks."

My grandmother Maude was a Scottish woman, and no one knew anything else about her or cared to ask; those who did would be answered with an icy, silent glare. If she had a family, they never came to visit, and she received no letters during her adult life. Her daughter's self-centred youth blocked the desire to understand her mother, and she could not see beyond the surface of her mother's constant irritability.

Maude's face gradually creased with the lines, giving her a permanent frown. Her aquiline nose gave her a haughty look, slightly softened when her brown curly hair would escape a bobby pin and a stray errant curl would dance for a while on her cheeks. The neighbours thought she was a snob and therefore could not be Australian. Behind her back they called her "sergeant major with a plum in her mouth". Her figure had been matronly even when she was a young girl, but it was compensated by her beautiful full bosom. All her life she walked erect, proud of her best physical endowment.

Every year in January she would buy a dress for herself and her daughter, choosing fine material from Mark Foy's department store. The dresses would last until the next year, despite daily wearing. Maude would cleverly create a different look with a brooch or lace collar for weddings or funerals. George gave her his whole pay packet every Friday, and she paid the weekly rent on the little house, gave George a meagre allowance, and saved the rest. The few shillings she gave George was certainly not enough to get drunk, but he managed to do so in spite of it by helping Pat in the cleaning of the pub on week-ends. Pat paid him with free beer every weeknight before six o'clock.

Proper English was important to Maude, who gave the impression that she was well bred, never swearing, and refusing to talk like those around her. When greeted with a "G'day, luv", she would answer with "Good morning" or Good afternoon" in a corrective tone, gazing past her greeter. She had stopped engaging in trite conversation many years before and refused to succumb to the neighbourhood around her, saying that the term "Aussie battler" was wasted on those people who always found the money for beer and cigarettes. "Pull up your boot straps," she would say, "and you won't be battling." She could not join in with the other women on the street who called themselves battlers. They hung over the fence every day, gossiping and giggling at her and referring to her as "bloody Queen Mary over there".

Accepting her circumstances—married to a drunk and with a child to whom she had difficulty showing affection—she cleaned, cooked, made the best of a postman's meagre pay, and refused to believe this was her station in life. Her presence in her daughter's and husband's life was mixed with an air of superiority, as if she was just an observer passing by and her life was a chore that she viewed with martyred dignity.

Maude did not understand the bond between her husband and their adopted daughter. She was not jealous; she just could not fathom why he could not see that Peggy was turning out wild. He seemed blind to every bad thing their daughter did. Peggy had been sneaking out at ten o'clock at night since she was fourteen years old. It was left up to Maude to discipline her. "Spare the rod, spoil the child" she would tell George if he woke from his drunken sleep as his beloved daughter was sneaking back in the house.

"She's sneaking out of the window every night, and you do nothing about it," Maude would complain.

"She's a good girl. She'll be right, luv, leave her alone."

Maude then would tell George that he would be sorry someday. The argument eventually would end as most of their arguments ended, with Maude bringing up George's time in France during the war.

"Why did you ever come back to Australia?" she'd ask. "You should have stayed in France with your girlfriend, Fifi." (This was a name Maude had made up because it was French and she thought it sounded rather "tarty".) No one ever knew if it was true that George had had a girlfriend during in France, but he did speak lovingly and longingly, with a far-away look in his eyes, of France and the French people.

Whenever they fought about France, they were man and woman with flickers of old jealousies and passion, a brief, pleasurable respite from the antics of their wayward daughter and the unwitting asexual drifting of their life together.

Crouching down, his small shoulders hunched, he would lift his trouser legs up to his knees. Baring his skinny white legs, singing and dancing around her in a circle, searching for the slightest hint of a smile. He was a mischievous elf circling his wife, looking for his pot of gold—a flicker of amusement in her eyes.

Mademoiselle from Armentieres, parlez-vous,
Mademoiselle from Armentieres, parlez-vous,
Mademoiselle from Armentieres, she hasn't been kissed in forty years,
Hinky dinky, parlez-vous.

Once, he thought he had seen her smile while he was hopping in circles around her, trying to make eye contact, but then he realized it was the start of a grimace of disgust and sadness.

"You better not be hopping around here like a no-hoper when that daughter of yours is going out every night, probably off with some Yank." In one sentence, she had won control, changing his brief feeling of hope and merriment to despair.

George had met Maude at a local dance, and they married before George went off to France. They didn't give a thought to the notion that they were not compatible, as their judgment was veiled by excitement and urgency of patriotic duty. Thrifty and clever enough to stretch a mailman's pay, they were still renting a tiny old house behind a box factory many years later. She was different person in those early years, young and filled with silly notions of how her life would be—a nice house and garden, books to read, and maybe a piano in the parlour. Something was missing in her imaginary idea of marriage, and she realized many years later that her dream never included the vision of a husband and children; they were blank faces, ghosts in her dreams, not worthy of names or faces.

Her life found its own level of comfort when she escaped to her dreams of someday living a solitary life. People spoke of the returning soldiers, saying, "They are never the same after the war," but Maude believed her husband was the same. He hadn't seen much fighting—maybe a few skirmishes in France, but the slaughter at Gallipoli was over when he joined. Maude believed people made this excuse for their weakness of character and they should "pull up their bootstraps" again. Had she, by some miracle, been able to look into the future without the obstruction of youthful optimism, her destiny would have been clear. George would be a drunk, and she would live in a rented house in Irish Town all her life. When the doctor said she was barren it did not upset her like it did George. She had never wanted children, but who could admit to not wanting children to anyone but yourself? Every woman was supposed to want children, but it was an instinct that she did not have or desire.

Four years after they were, married George talked about visiting an orphanage to inquire about adopting a baby. He thought that not having a baby must be the reason his wife never laughed or made friends with the other women, who always were laughing and hanging over the back fence, shouting at each other as they hung out a clothesline full of nappies.

The woman in charge of the orphanage said yes, there was one baby available for adoption, a nice, placid, pretty child with red hair. The mother was not married and refused to give information as to who the father was, but even if she had, she couldn't be believed anyway—she had a silver plate in her head as a result of a riding accident, and this had made her a little "well … insane, actually". In 1922 adopting, a bastard child with an unknown father and a mother whose morals were loosened by a piece of metal inside her head might have seemed a risk to most, but not to my grandparents. Maude refused to believe what some people said, that mental illness could be passed on to the child "through the blood". She saw this child—a child that no one wanted because of some ignorant superstition—as a challenge to her own intelligence and competence. In a quest to prove her point, if only to herself, she and George completed the adoption and took the child home; Maude took care of her new daughter's needs with the same efficiency as she did when peeling the potatoes. Although it was Maude who changed the dirty nappies and stayed up nights when the child was sick, this child, in her older years, always stood up for her father, and it seemed that the two of them always shut Maude out of their lives. It was true that she couldn't show affection, not in the way other people did, by kissing and hugging, but she kept a clean house without any outside help and stretched the measly few bob that was extra after paying rent and buying groceries. That was all she could do—and that should have been good enough. "Words are cheap," she always said when feeling unappreciated by her husband and daughter.

George and his mate Mick met when they served with the Fifty-sixth Battalion in France—George, as a fresh recruit; Mick, as one who survived the last days of Gallipoli. After the war, the only time they saw each other was when they assembled to begin the march down George Street every year for the parade. Mick never returned to his country town after the war; he settled in a small flat in Sydney's eastern suburbs, working as a conductor on the trains. He never married, and he drank only when he was with my grandfather reminiscing about the war. Mick always wore the same blue suit, shiny from years of steam-pressing for funerals, weddings, and ANZAC Day. He was over six feet tall and thin, with blue-grey eyes and a perpetual smile on his long, gaunt face. His head was always topped with his wide-brimmed grey Stetson. He seemed to delight in tipping his hat to the women he passed on his daily routine, and maybe this was the real reason he was never without his hat, or as he called it, "my lantern". Tipping his hat to women as they passed by on the street, standing when a lady came into the room, and being mindful of his language were gentlemanly gestures that proved to those around Mick (but mostly to himself) that being a gentleman had nothing to do with having money or coming from a so-called "good family".

George was five foot six. Years of living in this sun-blistered land with his Irish skin had gnawed at his face, painting it red and raw. His small nose between his weary, grey-hazel eyes was tinged with veins from drinking too much or from the sun, perhaps both. He wore a suit and tie every day, winter and summer. He wore the same black suit not only to weddings and funerals and on ANZAC Day but also to the pub, the butcher shop, and on Easter—and on the only time he attended church, midnight Mass on Christmas. He would wear a suit until it had holes and was so frayed that Maude's darning needle could not grab at a starting point in the cloth for a patch, even though in her thriftiness she had become an expert weaver. He would buy the exact same suit at Gowings and wear it for the next two years. George's only greeting to the women he passed on the street was "G'day, missus", if he recognized them, and his everyday speech in anyone's company consisted of the words bludger, bloody, and bugga; he used the words so often that eventually he became unaware that their place should be outside the fence of everyday acceptable conversation.

George had left Australia just before Christmas in 1915, shiny and eager, when he scrambled up the gangplank with hundreds of young soldiers on the ship bound for exotic places, like Turkey and France.

They were excited by this adventure and buoyed by the euphoria of invincibility only found in youth, blind optimists, and fools. He and his fellow passengers were Australian, and that meant they could not be beat. "Two-bob tourists" they were called by the Australians left behind, who saw this opportunity as a chance for their out-of-work boys to be paid for an exciting travel adventure. "It will be over by Christmas" they said. The two-bob tourists returned years later, with a spent boyhood and old eyes. They had fought side-by-side in France and had seen bloodshed for reasons they would silently question for the rest of their lives—but only to themselves or in conversation with each other.

Mick woke every night with the same recurring nightmare—the bodies of his mates were piled on top of each other in the shape of the Egyptian pyramid that had shadowed his camp while they waited to fight the Turks. His hands trembled and the sweat ran down the back of his neck, the bed soaked with dread that it might not be a dream and that he was back there, shooting at the endless stream of unflinching Turks who just kept coming. The nightly tremors never left him. George and Mick never spoke of their personal feelings—it was perceived as weak and not fitting talk. They always presented the stoic Australian persona. Towards the end of their life, they occasionally strayed from this national ideology and sought each other as friends whom they could trust with their deepest thoughts. Mick would admit in later years that the reason he never returned to his country town to marry his sweetheart was because of the embarrassment of the nightly drenched bed.

The two men always marched together as an affirmation of their silent bond, born many years before in France. It was suggested one year that Mick go to the back row of the parade and march with his taller fellow veterans for a better-looking parade, made more uniform by the levels of their height. "Little blokes in the front and taller in the back" the young parade organizer ordered. Mick, all the while sporting that perpetual smile, punched the poor, unwitting fellow, knocking him off his feet while the band hurriedly started the trumpets, drowning out the commotion.

"Bless 'em all, bless 'em all, bless 'em all,
The long, the short, and the tall,
Bless all the sergeants and WO1s.

So Mick and George marched in the front row for many years, with Mick's tall frame casting a shadow over his little mate George.

My mother always stood in the crowd, waving the Australian flag, cheering on her father and his towering friend. On the morning of the parade, George would tell his daughter that he would look for her in front of whatever landmark there was along the parade route. She would sit in the gutter, waving the Australian flag, and when the little soldier with his lanky mate was in her sight she would shout "Dadda, over here! Dadda!" unembarrassed by her enthusiasm, yelling louder till she caught his proud eyes, and he waved back.

After each Anzac Day Parade, Maude's orders not to bring Mick home were forgotten.

"Come on, Mick," George would say, "have tea with me and the missus." But my grandmother's unwelcome demeanour extended throughout her home. Always dark inside, the small weatherboard cottage with its corrugated iron roof and picket fence was as uninviting as kissing her cold, pursed lips. The curtains were never open; they were drawn to keep out the brilliant Australian sun—and to send a message that the rare visitor was not welcome. After Mick's polite greeting to his old friend's wife, both men would walk through the kitchen on their way to the back yard. They would pass the usual ANZAC day fare of simmering corned beef and cabbage boiling too long on the old coal stove. The narrow backyard was more comfortable and welcoming than the dark cold house. It was utter chaos and gloomy charm, with its broken brick path, dilapidated clothesline, a passion-fruit vine struggling to hug the dunny, and a yellow-crested cockatiel that was very originally named "Cocky".

"Hello, Cocky. Hello, Cocky" the poor bird would repeat over and over, when not screeching and running up and down the sides of his cage, his grey, leathered claws clenching and rattling the steel bars. Cocky never wavered in his innate attempt to escape the backyard slum for the open bush where he belonged.

"All those poor buggas, Mick. Was it worth it?" George asked.

"They said it would be over by Christmas, but that bloody Fisher promised our last man and our last shilling," Mick answered.

"And they almost got it."

"Over by Christmas," Mick scoffed. "Those pommies knew it wouldn't be over by bloody Christmas."

George nodded. "It was over by Christmas—yer Christmas four bloody years later!"

"Dunno, mate... well, we did get a letter signed from the king."

"Bloody pommy poofta," George spat out.

"We were stupid, George, thinking that it would be the last war. The 'war of wars' they called it."

"And now we are in another war, and the bloody Yanks are here. Cocky bastards, those Yanks. You watch—if we do win this bloody war, they will say they won it."

"Well, mate, Australia wasn't doing too good till they came into it. The Japs had their eyes on us; they were on their way."

"We woulda been right, Mick. You watch, Mick—they'll make us pay. We'll end up kissing America's arse."

Mick shook his head. "I dunno, mate, probably won't be around to see it."

"Well, I dunno, either. As long as they stay away from my Peggy; I don't trust them. It's true what they say about those bludgers—they're overpaid, oversexed, and over here, and here they are in Sydney, walking around like bloody galahs."

In 1942 George marched in the ANZAC Day parade in Sydney for the last time. Two weeks later he passed away in the backyard dunny; he had been there all night. It was not old war injuries that killed him, or the booze, or the leftover bacon fat that he ate every morning on his toast. He died of a broken heart when his adopted daughter—the daughter who led him every night out of the dunny to the tea table; the daughter who stood in the crowd, waving to him on anzac day; the daughter who promised him that she would never marry a bludger—got on the train that morning and left for Queensland to marry an American sailor.

U.S. Navy dance, 1943, Australia
"My mother and father", centre

2
THE TROC

After six months, a respectably enough time to mourn her husband, my grandmother began to enact her secretly repressed dream of living alone, without a drunken leprechaun dancing around her or a resentful daughter insisting that her father's tea should be served hot and cheerfully, no matter in what condition or what time he came home. She packed her cut-glass vase, embroidered pillowcases, and crocheted doilies—items that had been patiently waiting for a chance at a refined life; reminders that once in her younger life, there had been a dream—into the boot of a taxi and then took the taxi over the harbour bridge to her new home in Neutral Bay. Ironically, the southern Zetland and the northern suburb of Neutral Bay were the same distance from the city but in opposite directions. The southern side, with its factories, stables, and tanneries, contrasted the north, with its leafy streets and mansions that were visible from the water's edge. The Aborigines from the north called the area across Sydney Cove "warung", meaning "the other side", while the same word was used by the Aborigines from the south to refer to the north. Class distinction was not in the Aborigine language; it was simply the other side of the water, subject to where they happened to be standing at the time. Judgment of a man's merit by the accident of noble birth and a prestigious address was exclusively a white man's perception, introduced and presently sustained by the descendants of Australia's early European settlers.

Second-hand furnishing and the rent on the little house in Neutral Bay were funded by the widow's pension, pennies saved over many years, and my grandmother's unwavering thrift. Her life settled in to the routine of polishing her furniture which would never to be enjoyed by any visitors. Her unfriendly coldness had become deeply imbedded after so many years of practice, and she was unable shed it in a fifteen-minute taxi ride, albeit to a "better" address. The house came with roses, their planting and early nurturing a bequeathed gift from the last aesthete occupant. They would add a soft ornamental contrast between the cold, grey solidity of the square stone house and nature's frail, unmatched beauty. The home itself was square, with a centre entrance, and built before the larger and more distinctive Australian Federation era, when architecture turned towards embracing the Australian climate and lifestyle and withdrew from such dark English-style buildings and convict-built cottages. In order to blend with the more visually pleasing Federation homes that circled its perimeter, with their leadlight windows and fretwork, the house on Undercliff Street had been gussied up over the years, A veranda had been added, with wooden handrails and tiling on the floor, probably by the same family whose visual journey was not complete without the final icing on their reinvented cake: the addition of ten rose bushes. As is not uncommon for women liberated from life's dictated duties, my grandmother finally found a passion: an unexpected wonder and love for gardening. Early in the morning she would be out in the front of the house, tending the rose bushes, three each side of the centre gate inside the iron fence. In the cooler afternoon, with the north-facing backyard, she would find renewed energy for her task and bring out old, sturdy tools she had found in the backyard wash shed.

She was happiest when pruning, watering, and digging in the dirt. The roses in the back were not the full, double-bloomed, red English roses that graced the front fence, poking their red cheeky faces through the iron slats to peek out on the quiet street. The backyard roses were climbers. Wilder, they needed more guidance, and she stretched their long canes over trellises, the stone wash house, and the outdoor building that housed the toilet (it was not called a dunny over this side of the harbour). Without the broken concrete, factory and stable smells, and Cocky, with his endless screams for liberation, the backyard was quiet and peaceful, in contrast to her life over the past thirty years. If only her daughter had been like the climbing rose; if only my grandmother had been able to intersect her daughter's wild spirit and guide her towards a better path, as she did the climbing roses. But her beautiful adopted baby had grown more like the uncontrollable weeds that popped up every day, sturdy and belligerent.

It was a short walk from her house to the ferry that carried her across the harbour on a delightful five-minute trip to the city. Spending very little money, she would walk through the shops her keen fashion eye, looking for the inexpensive brooch, necklace, or lace collar to elevate her basic navy dress to the current styles. Her pride was the fashionable red fox stole that she wore around her neck, the poor dead animal dressing up her plain black coat, its glass-eyed head hanging over her ample bosom, feet dangling in utter submission. Its free wild life had been given up for such a fickle purpose: the short life of women's fashion. The simpler the better, she had told her daughter many times, trying to impart her fusion of thrift and prudence; this philosophy would prove to be her one success with her daughter. The weekly excursions to the city included a stop at Sydney's Mitchell Library in a quest for more knowledge on her newly acquired gardening passion. She knew that it was beneficial to give plantings nourishment by adding tea leaves and eggshells to the soil, but surely that was too simple for something as complicated as growing English roses in an Australia's hot climate. Because my grandmother no longer had to worry about a husband whose only aspiration was to sing melancholy songs (often with a degree of gloom, depending on how much he'd had to drink) or concern herself with an errant daughter who was off with some American in Queensland, she would enjoy worrying over whether her roses were browning prematurely in the front yard or if the canes on the backyard climbers were leafless and spindly. Her answers were always found at the library, and even though most of the books were written to address the problems of English gardens, she made clever adjustments for climate and availability. Amused by her welcome dilemma in horticulture, she remembered the never-ending supply of "gold" near her old Zetland home: well-rotted animal manure. All those years it was right there, and she took it for granted, repulsed with the smell of horse stables. Now, she coveted the idea of having a big pile of horse dung plopped right there in her backyard.

Catching the ferry back to Neutral Bay at the end of the day, she would look up at the splendid, stately homes of Kirribilli House and the neighbouring Admiralty House, satisfied to be living close to such splendid homes.

My grandmother Maude—the years alone

Admiralty House, built in the late 1840s, was purchased by the New South Wales government in 1885 and was used as an official residence for the admiral who commanded the British Squadron in Australia. Due to many alterations and additions by various previous owners, the front rooms were given good views down the harbour, making it easy to spot advancing enemy ships. Kirribilli House was built next door in 1855 and eventually became the property of the Commonwealth Government of Australia, to be used as the official residence of the prime minister. Both magnificent homes are across the water from the Opera House just east of the north side of the Sydney Harbour Bridge.

Mum has said that my grandmother must have been getting lonely, because when my mother wrote that she was going to have a baby, and that the U.S. Navy was sending her husband off to the

Philippines and that she would like to come back to Sydney to have her baby, Maude answered immediately by urgent telegram:

SEND DATE AND TRAIN ARRIVAL TIME.

It was 1944, and although the war wasn't won until 1945, Australia's sense of threat had somewhat subsided. Most Australians were cautious in their sense of priorities about the war, tempered by lessons learned in World War I. This time there was no rush to enlist; it was a wiser nation, hardened by sorrow and sores not healed by blind trust in the mother country. The government moved more slowly in balancing its own national needs with duty to Britain. The threat to the shores of Australia was real for much of the six years of the duration of the war. This threat was heightened by Japan's entry into the war in December 1941 and Germany's advancing strength in Europe. In May 1942, armed forces from the United States, Australia, and New Zealand intercepted a Japanese fleet in the Battle of Coral Sea, preventing the landing of Japanese troops on the south coast of New Guinea and, ultimately, ending the threat to the shores of Australia and New Zealand.

There were many casualties in the Pacific, but my father, stationed on an aircraft carrier, unfortunately was not one of them. If he had been killed, I could have carried the image throughout my life of a young American hero who took a part in saving Australia—my mother would have received some stipend from the American government—and she would have shed a million fewer tears over her lifetime. But most of all, his death would have prevented some of the evil he was to impart.

Arriving at Central Station from Queensland, my mother did not expect the welcome she received from the woman she had left a few years earlier after writing only a simple note:

Dear Mumma and Dadda,

Gone to Queensland to marry Hart. Don't worry; I will write soon.

Your loving daughter,

Peggy

Although she looked out the window on the train from Queensland, Peggy, my mother, had not taken much notice of how the landscape changed as the train got closer to each station. The small towns, with their weatherboard cottages, schools, churches, butcher shops, and corner pubs, dotted the terrain all the way down the coast. Some of the scenery was barren red earth with scraggly gum trees, tinder waiting for the inevitable surrender to nature's fiery cleansing. She remained deep in thought and hypnotized by the blur of the landscape that whizzed by as the train got closer to Sydney, with its more modern brick homes tucked between greener trees. Questions entered her mind, questions she hadn't thought of until now, and she sobbed. Would her mother blame her for her father's death? Would she be welcome to stay in her mother's new home? If the war did not end soon, Peggy realized that she would have to find work, but who would look after her baby?

When she was alone in her Queensland flat in MacKay, Peggy often thought about her real mother—her birth mother. She was raised to believe that she was Maude and George's natural child, and she probably would never have known the truth if it hadn't been for Harry, a younger cousin, who ran up to her on the school playground when she was twelve. "My mother said you're adopted," he announced. "Auntie Maude is not your real mother." And so she waited until she was alone in the house, and she went to the tin box at the back of the wardrobe, the box that she thought only contained things like her father's papers from the war. She found her proof and ran to tell her friend, waving the papers in the air.

"I found them, Gladys," she cried out.

"So what? That's not important," Gladys responded. "I told my mother that you were looking for the papers, and she said that a lot of people can have children, but not everyone can be a mother or a father and take care of their children. So put the papers back, and we'll bash up Harry tomorrow at school."

"Why didn't you tell me I was adopted?" she asked Maude and George later that day.

George said, "She couldn't take care of you, and we could. We love you, stinkpot." He used his name for her when he wanted to see her laugh.

Maude said nothing to her daughter except, "Go and set the table for tea"

Separated by a playground and tennis court, the boy's school, down the hill from the girl's school, let out fifteen minutes after the girls school did. Gladys and Peggy waited for Harry behind the boy's toilet. Harry went home that afternoon with a bloody nose, a black eye, a torn school uniform, and a missing tie, along with a promise that there was a spell over him, and a witch would come and take him away in the middle of the night. In the years that followed when the families met at the occasional funerals, weddings, or birthday parties, neither Harry nor his mother ever said anything about the day Peggy and Gladys took their revenge. The incident had confirmed what they all knew all along that "what's in the blood will come out". The adopted daughter of Maude and George was a crazy girl, and so they kept their distance.

The only U.S. Navy chaplain available was not Catholic but a Methodist. Even if he had been Catholic, he was against these quick marriages and made it a point to say so to all future brides. "You young ladies don't know what lies ahead of you. Wait until the war is over, and then he can come back to marry you." He said this, knowing it was not likely to happen when the world was back to normal. His advice was dismissed by couples who were caught in a time when the desire to touch and bed down meant you were in true love, and therefore, you must get married. They needed to have a respectable label like "Mrs." before giving themselves permission to do what they wanted to do more than anything in life—to lie together in bed forever. This passionate desire was a cruel curse designed by nature to ensure human propagation; its euphoria dissipated rationality during the urgent times of war.

Peggy and Hart had found a cranky old Catholic priest to marry them. Gladys came up from Sydney to be her bridesmaid, and they borrowed a witness from the Navy cafeteria. The marriage was mixed—Peggy was Catholic; Hart was Protestant—despite belief in the same God and the mutual Jesus connection.—so the wedding had to take place "behind the altar". Only the elite (meaning both man and woman were Catholic) were allowed in front of the tabernacle, an ornate box dressed in satins that held the consecrated host, the body of Christ—but apparently a different Christ from the Protestants' Christ.

Counselling before the marriage was mandatory. The old priest grunted mostly, probably knowing that any lectures would be a waste of his weary breath. He knew which couples, over the years, listened to his spiritual guidance, and his experience told him this couple would not be one of them. Hart, my father, was told that the children from the marriage would have to be brought up as Catholics. After agreeing to this, he and Peggy were allowed to marry in the lovely church, however they were barred from marrying in front of the tabernacle and the vows were required to be said behind the altar.

"I felt like a nigger," Hart told his father years later.

Peggy would have walked right past the thin, sunburned woman standing at the end of the train platform, except that she recognized the familiar black coat, topped with a dead fox. Maude looked older, with soft folds of skin hanging from her chin. The round, stern face that Peggy remembered, always unyielding, refusing any glimpses of joy, had changed; Maude's eyes now seemed to hold a secret contentment. No words were spoken between the two women as they walked through the commotion of Sydney's Central Station, with its din of braking steam engines and the loud, excited shouts of passengers coming and going. "Meet me under the clock at Central" became a safe mantra for Sydneyites to lessen the chance of losing loved ones—there was no mistaking that clock because of its huge size and its position, suspended in the main thoroughfare. At any time, day or night, there would be a group of people with their eyes searching the crowd, while waiting under that big clock at Sydney's Central Railway station. Maude reached over and took her daughter's hand, squeezing her fingers in silent affection.

Peggy opened her coat and patted her swollen belly with a nervous laugh. "Remember, Mumma, what you used to say? 'Always buy a good coat, and it will hide a multitude of sins', although I know you meant a shabby dress."

"You're married. It's not a sin; it's a blessing."

The two settled in together with mutual tolerance. Peggy, somewhat tempered by a newfound humility, was grateful that she was no longer alone in a flat in MacKay. She reunited with her friend Gladys, although she couldn't understand Maude's desire to leave Sydney's south for these unfamiliar surroundings.

"Why did you move here, Mumma?"

"To be near the water and the ferries and away from the factories," Maude answered.

"'Struth, it's so bloody far to get over to Gladys; a ferry and then a tram," Peggy complained.

"This is where I live now," Maude said evenly, "and you are welcome to live here, have the baby, and stay here as long as you want."

I was born three months later at the Mater Misericordia Hospital in North Sydney. My name was supposed to be Diana Maude—Diana upon my father's insistence (where he got that name, I do not know), and Maude after my grandmother. "Diana Maude" was changed, thank God, by divine intervention, when a nursing nun at the Mater Hospital said that neither of those names belonged to saints, and if I didn't have a saint's name, my life would be doomed and entry to heaven certainly questionable. "Call her Mary," the nun suggested, going right to the top of the chain for female saints, so in compromise it became Diana Marie.

Mum & Me, Sydney 1944

Australia's National Security Act of 1939 implemented controls that would affect many Australian lives; it gave the Commonwealth government the power to make laws in areas that were previously off-limits to the Commonwealth because of the Australian Constitution. These laws included the prosecution of about one thousand conscientious objectors, the formation of a Women's Land Army, banning the Communist Party and the Australian First Movement for opposing the war, and setting women's pay rates at almost (heaven forbid) men's levels. There was also rationing of clothing, footwear, tea, butter, and sugar. While not having silk stockings was a blow to some women's quest to enhance the look of their legs while wearing the fashionable short skirts of the day, they imitated the seam of a stocking by drawing a line up the back of their legs with eyebrow pencils, refusing to accept defeat in what, to some, was the heaviest hardship of the war. They could go without tea and butter, but fashion—well, that was another thing altogether. While my grandmother even rationed the rations with programmed thriftiness, my mother, married to an American serviceman and having access for a year to the post exchange, the U.S. military supermarket, brought back to Sydney such luxuries as silk stockings, sweets, and tea, all hoarded in four suitcases. Shortly after my birth, her figure recovered to its pre-maternity svelte look, my mother went to work in the bindery at the *Sun* office, a Sydney publishing company that printed magazines and weekly inserts. That year, every woman on the bindery floor, young or old, hemmed her dresses a little shorter to show off her coveted silk stockings with real seams running up the back of the legs, compliments of the United States Navy.

My grandmother moved my pram around the small yard every day, following the sun's movement in her calculated attempt to rotate me between the natural vitamins bestowed by sunshine and the comforting repose of shade, as she cooed and fussed over her obedient roses. Both of these charges she carried out with quiet joy, basking with satisfaction at this time of her life, the years of worry behind her, the Japanese threat to Australia diminished, and the husband who gave her nothing but embarrassment gone forever.

Despite the hardship of rations—one egg per person per week, no petrol for most, and the scarcity of clothing and building materials—it was the time of most abundance for the two woman who were then my whole family. The U.S. Navy, not wanting any problems with the Australian wives of their newly married personnel, made sure that pay checks were monitored, and my father regularly sent money. This money, coupled with my mother's wages and Grandma's frugality, meant that we were now rich, in comparison to the past. More crystal-cut glass came into the house, along with an English mantle clock—its Westminster chime could be heard as far away as the back shed, melodiously bestowing a sense of Old World permanence in this tiny rented house. Anthony Horderns furniture store delivered a big, bulky, brown tweed lounge suite that took up most of the space in the tiny living room, leaving no path to walk without the constantly stubbing one's toes. My mother would climb over the couch to get from one end of the room to the other.

Sydney's nightlife was excited by a sense of heady urgency; the uncertainty of war had fuelled a sexually free attitude to enjoy the present moment. Laughter and a quest for more laughter prevailed in the survival instincts of the human spirit. While Australia did not see the devastation from war that other countries experienced, there were times when the threat of invasion seemed imminent, and it was then that concerns and fears could be danced away, briefly, to the non-stop music of swing and other popular music played by talented local bands. Air-raid wardens enforced black-outs at night, prohibiting any street lights and ensuring that black curtains covered the inside of the windows so that no glimmer of light could be seen from the air. While the Red Cross hosted dances and the sophisticated Sydney nightclubs flourished, some clubs, such as Prince's and Romano's, were open only to American and Australian officers. My mother, Peggy, and my father, Hart, a petty officer, met at the famed Trocadero, previously an elegant venue for a more refined patron but now packed every night, after being requisitioned as a recreational centre for all Australian and American non-commissioned officers. The pre-war days of genteel afternoon tea dances were gone. There were many fights between the Americans, with wads of money and cigarettes falling from their pockets, and the resentful, low-paid Australian soldiers. The Trocadero was reduced at times to unruly mayhem, while the orchestra didn't need a signal from the bandleader to quickly lower their beat, changing from swing music to some American song before the police arrived.

Give my regards to Broadway,
Remember me to Herald Square,
Tell all the gang at Forty-second Street
That I will soon be there.

Hearing the songs of home would calm the Americans and cause them to become sad and reflective, two characteristics not conducive to brawling.

The stars at night
Are big and bright
Deep in the heart of Texas.
The prairie sky
Is big and high …

Finishing their late shift in the bindery, Peggy and her friends would take off the uniform they wore over their dresses, pin up their hair over their ears (one roll of twisted hair tucked and pinned on the nape of the neck), share the latest shade of lipstick, douse themselves with perfume, and burst from the building, fresh as young daisies, headed for the "Troc" with excited chatter. While no drinking was allowed in the Trocadero, several invitations to share a bottle were offered on the streets by small groups of American sailors who were hovering in doorways of closed shops or back lanes or just sitting on the curbs.

Always the sensible one of the two, Gladys would gently remind her old friend, "You're married now and a mother. And your poor husband is off fighting somewhere in the Pacific."

"I'm just having a good time after working all day," Peggy would tell her. "Besides, I'm not going to be left out of the fun." Being married to an American, Peggy thought, made her more worldly and able to look out for her friends. Except for the lights searching the sky, the harbour would be dark by the time the last Neutral Bay ferry would carry her home across the bay. She was exhausted from a night of dancing—and from taking a swig of liquor in dark doorways while playfully (or forcefully) dodging the amorous intentions of young men so far from home. Many of these young men, who were trying to forget the deaths of their soldier brothers while hanging on to their own lives and dreams, found themselves thrust in a country on the other side of the world, so far away from their families.

No words were spoken between Maude and Peggy about the late hours spent away from her baby. My grandmother may have just been too tired, or perhaps she knew that her daughter's carefree days in Sydney would soon end. She had met my father briefly when he came to Sydney on leave and stayed with them for two days. She called him "Slick"; she knew that the two of them had been smoking out in the back laundry, and she observed the fact that he had not paid much attention to the baby, calling her "fish face".

"Look, she moves her mouth like a fish," he'd say. And when he left, Maude knew beyond any doubt that her daughter's life with

"Slick" would be filled with heartache.

Now with a baby and knowing that eventually she would be moving to America, my mother felt a need to see and visit her "real" mother, the mother she had found out about from her cousin Harry ten years earlier. She would go look for her searching the streets of Marrickville for the address listed on the papers in the biscuit tin at the back of the wardrobe. The wardrobe had been moved over to Neutral Bay, but the tin was still there.

"You have to come with me, Glad," Peggy said when she told her friend about going to visit her real mother at the sanatorium.

"What do you want to do this for, Peggy? You'll just upset yourself. Now come on, luv, be sensible." Her argument was futile, however, and they went on a rainy April morning.

The old ***Sun*** office bindery, Anzac Day Parade
My mother, centre, right-hand waving

Nellie Kennedy, Peggy's birth mother, and my real grandmother, lived in a world known only to her; it consisted of her twitching, screaming loudly and then whispering gibberish as if she was a passerby quietly scolding the screaming woman who was herself. There was no recognition of her daughter, granddaughter, or anyone. My mother visited her every two weeks, and if Maude knew it, she did not let on. Nellie would just stare blankly at Peggy between outbursts of repeatedly screaming, "*Where's my tea? Where's my tea? Where's my tea?*" The story was that she had fallen off a horse during her pregnancy, and doctors had put a silver plate in her head. With the rudimentary knowledge of mental health in the 1920s, it was believed that insanity could be transmitted to the foetus.

The story about the horse always seemed suspect to me and rather dramatic. My family research in later years revealed to me only that Nellie was not married when she was pregnant, and there was no record of the baby's father. On one occasion back in 1945 my mother got permission from the director of the home where Nellie resided to take her out for the day, just the two of them, mother and daughter. After dressing her mother in the old coat and hat that she found in her room closet, the two were off for the day, after being given a warning from the nurse that Nellie should never be allowed to wander out of my mother's sight. Perhaps my mother had hoped there would be a change in her mother, and maybe a possible small hint of recognition and mental clarity that might come from being away from institutional confinement. As they strolled through David Jones Department Store, Nellie grabbed boxes of handkerchiefs and tried to stuff them under her coat. Peggy grabbed them away from her mother and putting them back on the shelf, saying, "C'mon now, don't do that. We're going to go for a nice cup of tea and scones."

Walking through Hyde Park, Nellie broke away from her daughter's grip and started to undress while climbing into the park's Archibald Fountain. Feeling defeated, my mother took Nellie back to Marrickville in a taxi. She kissed her mother at the door and said goodbye forever through her tears as she handed Nellie back over to a nurse.

Japan surrendered, and the war ended in August 1945. Over 39,000 Australians had given their lives to this war, with over 30,000 taken prisoner by the Japanese and Germans. Within a few months, we had passage, paid by the American government, to join my father, who had been returned to the U.S. and was now completing his Navy commitment by recruiting in his hometown of Wichita, Kansas.

"Mumma, I don't want to go to America," Peggy wailed.

"I blame that father of yours," Maude said. "He let you get away with everything. He never lifted a finger. You needed a good hiding, sneaking out to meet those Americans. I knew you were up to no good. Well, too late now, my girl; you've made your bed. You've got to do the right thing."

They stood on the dock, saying good-bye. Gladys was sobbing, and my grandmother's grim, round face was squeezed hard. Her teeth were clenched, and her eyes were narrowed almost shut in determination to stop the tears.

"I'll be back, Glad," Peggy insisted, "when Hart is finished with the Navy. We'll come back; you mark my words, Glad. Two bloody years, no longer. I'll be back."

"You might meet some Hollywood movie stars over there," Gladys said. "Get an autograph for me from Glenn Ford."

"I don't give a bugga about any bloody movie stars," Peggy told her. "We've got Chips Rafferty right here in Australia."

The Ship pulled away from the dock at Circular Quay and turned towards the Sydney Heads. Peggy looked up at the beloved bridge, remembering so many afternoons when she and her father had climbed the stairs to the top of the pylon for a breathtaking view of their beloved city. Then, looking back down to the wharf, she saw the only two people who made up her Australian family, their figures getting smaller and smaller. She couldn't look away; she feared they might disappear forever—Gladys, in a pale blue dress, a beacon in the crowd with her red curly hair, arm in arm with the woman wearing a black coat and a dead fox.

War Brides of World War 11 Leaving Australia on the SS. Lurline

Gladys, holding me on the day my mother and I left for America

3

VERY REVEREND RATBAG

The room was dark; the shifting sun beating outside at two o'clock in the afternoon could not even dance through a crack between the lace curtains, which were temporarily covered with the heavy, dark wool blankets. Two tables were placed together, end to end, in a small dining room that had not seen any actual dining in over five years.

"No reason to celebrate until Lionel comes home," Eunice had told her sister, Birdie. Reverend Glass said that it needed to be dark and quiet so that he could concentrate and open up his mind, as only then the spirits and the spirit world would feel welcome. Nine people gathered that day in this white California-style bungalow in Wichita, Kansas. The group consisted of five women—Eunice, Birdie, two women from the Evangelical Faith Community Church, and my mother, a recent arrival into this Midwest American family. The four men who joined them were my father; his father, Milton; Birdie's husband, who was always referred to (even in front of Birdie) as "slow-witted Roy"; and Mr. Donald Glass, a self-proclaimed psychic and evangelist, who had the God-given gift to deliver messages from the Promised Land, according to the article in the Evangelical Pentecostal Faith Community Church's paper that circulated in Oklahoma, Missouri, and Kansas. Eunice said they were so blessed to have this man as their visitor, and Birdie thanked her sister every day for her generosity in allowing this divine man to stay in Eunice's house while waiting for a message from—or even about—Lionel.

Birdie and Roy did not believe the telegram that informed them that their only son was missing in action in 1943. They would set a place for him every night at their dinner table, believing that someday, he would come home to them, as long as they had faith. Every knock on their door was answered with the heart-throbbing expectation that on the other side would be their blue-eyed, blond, handsome Lionel, grinning and ready to get back to work, side by side with his dad, in the backyard machine-repair shop. Eunice had offered her extra bedroom to Mr. Glass, knowing that while Birdie's house had two bedrooms, the empty bedroom was still waiting for

Lionel's return. High school banners and toy cars were waiting in the exact spot Lionel had left them, and for anyone, even the spiritually connected Mr. Donald Glass, to get into Lionel's bed and move those cars, even slightly, might disrupt the course of her son's journey home. Eunice had been aware of her younger sister's odd way of thinking since they were children. Birdie's had no friends except for Eunice, and when other children had tried to include her in games, she would stare at them and run off. Efforts to coax her sister socially over the years were met with a blank stare and with Birdie's returning to the comfort of her internal world.

"Say it's a nice day today, Birdie, if you can't think of anything to say. Just don't glare at people," Eunice would tell her sister without success. As a child, Birdie never touched her toys; she would count them over and over, her fingers pointing one inch away from the satin bride dolls or the furry bears. She was content to stay in her room, as if guarding her untouched toys from the outside world.

Eunice and Birdie's father had died when they were young, and their depressed mother ignored her children, leaving Eunice to worry alone about the strange evolving behaviour of her younger sister. Eunice gave her sister a reception at the church hall when she married Roy. Through the years, all of Lionel's parties, birthdays and his graduation, were held at Eunice's house. Eunice knew that her sister would not have come out of her bedroom if there were other people in her own house. Eunice prayed daily that Mr. Glass might be able to renew her sister's hope, a hope that she saw slowly dwindling as Birdie's odd behaviour accelerated, with more counting and pointing. A message from her sister's son Lionel through this Christian man might be the answer to all her prayers. If Lionel had been killed in the war and could talk to his mother through the reverend, then Birdie would know that some day she and Lionel would be together. Reverend Glass had the God-given gift and could contact the spirits who wandered between the sinners of this earth and the heavenly world of buttercups and sunshine.

When Eunice told Birdie about Mr. Glass and his "gift", she saw a light switch on in her sister's eyes.

Eunice then called Mr. Glass immediately to discuss the possibility of his visiting Wichita.

A woman answered the phone. "Yeah, whatta ya want?"

Eunice had second thoughts; this did not sound the way a Christian woman should talk. When Eunice told the woman that she had read a story about Mr. Glass's ability to contact the spirits and that her sister's son was missing in action, the woman's voice became soft and kind. She said she would have Mr. Glass call her back that night when he got home from visiting the poor brethren. The soft voice at the other end of the phone assured Eunice that although he would be tired after his compassionate day with the sickly, he would never be too tired to call a poor grieving aunt and mother of a boy who went to fight for the freedom of these great United States of America. Eunice hurried over to her sister's house to tell Birdie that Reverend Glass would be calling that night. Eunice, shaking her sister's shoulders in her excitement, God was finally leading her to her Lionel, and she could talk to her boy, wherever he is.

"Reverend Glass was born with a gift, and we are going to have him right here in our midst," Eunice said. "It's just for you, Birdie; I am doing this just for you, so I can see you happy again, like the night Lionel was born. Remember, Birdie? I was at your side that night, and I always will be."

That night, Mr. Glass returned the call. If Eunice had not known better, she would have thought that Mr. Glass was into the drink, but then, perhaps he was exhausted from all his good works. Mr. Glass said he would need to come to Kansas, walk around where Lionel had walked, visit his house, and get to know the family. And before he could come, he would need three hundred dollars for expenses and donations to the sick and the good works of his church. Eunice said she would have to talk to her husband, Milton, and her sister, Birdie, about the three hundred dollars. Mr. Glass said he could not 'pussyfoot around,' which Eunice thought seemed like a funny thing to say for a man with a great spiritual calling. He said he had a lot of people waiting to talk to their loved ones on the other side, but he would put her first, because Lionel had gone to fight for his country, and a family that is so unselfish as to give a boy to fight for the freedom of the these here great United States of America deserved to come first. Milton told his wife that Mr. Glass could come and stay if it would make her and Birdie happy. He knew Lionel was dead and would never return through a spiritual man's intervention, or even in a coffin. He knew that Lionel's body had been blown to bits—not even enough to scrape up in a little bag to send home. There would be no Lionel coming home, but for the first time in four years, Milton had seen the two sisters flutter with excitement, and he was not going to be the one to tell them that Lionel would never knock on the door again—or that they were being fools to believe in this con man. The light in Birdie had died when two men in the uniform stood at their doorway, following up on the telegram that Lionel was missing in action. He would try to keep these two women hopeful for as long as he could. He just didn't know how long this Mr. Glass could keep up the charade.

The next day, Birdie and Eunice were waiting for the Bank of America to open its doors. They withdrew three hundred dollars and walked fast up Euclid Street to the Western Union office and wired it off Mr. Donald Glass in Tallahassee Florida. Two months went by with no word from the great psychic spirit man. Birdie started counting dishes in her cupboard, pointing over and over, while Eunice had everyone at the Evangelical Pentecost Community Church pray for her to find Mr. Glass and Birdie's three hundred dollars. If that wasn't enough, their own son Hart, who was out in San Francisco and hopefully would stay there, had called to say he was bringing his newly arrived wife and baby home to stay with them while he found work "and got on his feet". As Eunice told it, he had met a woman in Australia—or was it Austria? She was not sure but hoped it was Austria, as she remembered from her school lessons that there was a country called Australia, and its people were wild and dark with mud in the creases of their leathered skin. They would not put it past Hart, though, to have married a wild muddy Australian; he was always embarrassing them. Before he joined the Navy, Eunice and Milton were always mortified in front of the neighbours when a police car, at least once a week, would pull up in front of their house, looking to ask Hart questions. It had started with missing bikes and cats when he was about ten years old, and then, when he was twelve, Mrs. Shaffer, a widow living behind Milton and Eunice, had seen him loitering around outside her kitchen. Later, her purse was missing, along with her only companion, Bonnie, her beloved poodle. This time the county sheriff had him; he had been seen when the Fuller Brush man, making a delivery, had walked to the back of the house to deliver brushes to Mrs. Shaffer and had been knocked off his feet when Hart ran out of the house, a black leather purse under one arm and a poodle under the other. Six months in the Christian Home for Wayward Boys did not purge him of the devil, as the pastor at the Evangelical Pentecost Community Church had assured Eunice and Milton would occur; instead, he had learned to be "slick" and how to outsmart the police and stay "one-step ahead of the sheriff", as my mother later would tell me. At nineteen he stole lightning rods from a warehouse and then, going farm to farm, sold them cheap along the desolate highways to unsuspecting farmers. Just before being arrested, he walked in to the recruiting office for the U.S. Navy. Everyone said this would make an honest man out of him: "The Navy will straighten him out." And both Milton and Eunice breathed a sigh of relief, except that he took his cousin Lionel with him.

After ten weeks had gone by since the day Eunice and Birdie wired the three hundred dollars to Reverend Glass in Tallahassee, a miracle occurred when he called Eunice's house on a Sunday night. He was sorry, but he hadn't had any way of getting in touch with them, as he had been called on by the Lord to work with sinners in Missouri, preaching the gospel and putting them on the right path. Now that their souls were saved, he could return to his ministry of contacting loved ones in the spirit world. In addition, Mr. Glass said that thanks to Birdie and Eunice's generosity and patience, souls were saved in Alabama. "Praise the Lord, dear woman, you will go straight to heaven, and, my dear woman, could you have your sister send another three hundred dollars?" Slow-witted Roy said no, absolutely not.

Reverend Glass decided to come anyway, and arrived looking grungy and oily, after two days on a bus. He was a tall, robust man, with thinning blond hair and a sharp nose. Over the years he had perfected a haughty bearing; holding his head back, he looked down his nose and spoke in a whisper. They were not to tell anyone he was there, he cautioned them. If anyone from the town knew who he was, given his reputation for tireless devotion to his lesser brethren, he would surely be called to another mission to preach and save souls. This would leave poor Birdie waiting once again for a message from Lionel. Eunice thought of her frail little sister, counting her dishes over and over and then walking into corners to stare at the wall, and who was now sitting in the backseat of the car, singing and humming.

"Rock of Ages, cleft for me. Let me hide myself in Thee. Hum-m-m … hum-m-m-m … Let me hide myself in Thee."

So nothing was said about who Reverend Glass was, except to say he was a friend of Milton's from Oklahoma and was staying with them until he got on his feet.

Mr. Donald Glass stayed for six months, and every morning, he wrote his dinner request on a note for Eunice to take to the Piggly Wiggly: steak, crab meat (yes, he would take the canned if it was the only one she could find), chocolates for his bedroom, and lots of lemons for fresh-squeezed lemonade.

When we arrived from Australia via San Francisco, Milton told the perturbed reverend that he would have to move into the smaller bedroom. "Those kids and the baby need the big bedroom. Now, I don't mind you staying here, hiding from who knows what and eating our food, as long as you respect our home. I don't believe that you or anyone else can talk to Lionel or spirits from heaven, and I believe you know that, but Eunice is happy just thinking that you can let them talk to her sister's boy. And right now, she sees that her sister is happy. You can stay as long as you can keep them in the dark about your scam, but you can't pull the wool over my eyes, mister, and you will do what I say."

Not a word was said in response from Mr. Glass. Needing to lie low a little while longer and not wanting any trouble, he moved his one suitcase quietly into the smaller bedroom.

My mother hated living in America. It wasn't a sudden shock to her; she knew she wouldn't like it. She had nothing against America or Americans personally, though they did go on about themselves a bit, she always said, waving their flags and saying they lived in the best country in the world. But it was only going to be for a short time, and she would do the right thing until her husband finished his duty in the Navy. Then they would go back to Australia forever. When they returned, he would get a good job and a house in Sydney, close to Gladys—maybe in Redfern, so they could be near the factories, walk to work, go to the pubs, and maybe join the Returned Soldiers League Club. If he found work in the country, he could have a shed in the backyard because she knew he could invent things; he was good with inventions. He could figure things out; electrician first class petty officer in the United States Navy, he was, she always said proudly. Maybe he would invent something big, and their children, of course, would be smart just like him and go to a boarding school, like all the other country children.

It had been a month earlier when the tugboat nestled up to the *Lurline,* dragging its eighteen thousand tons of bulk down the foggy San Francisco harbour, guiding it slowly until it nestled next to the cement wharf. The ship would rest for a week, and then the cables would lift anchors, and the ship would begin another trip down to the bottom of the world to fetch another batch of young, hopeful women.

"We're in America, girls!" This was the excited chatter of three hundred women who had shared ironing boards, pressing silk blouses, spitting on shoes, squirting "Evening in Paris" and "Apple Blossom" perfume at each other. ("Here, I'll give you a little squirt.") They changed nappies, slathered on red lipstick, and wiped infant vomit from the shoulder of stylish linen and shantung frocks. They all had imagined this day while crossing the Pacific and the way they would be greeted as they walked off the ship and into their new lives.

Women's lives in America were full of movie stars, shiny cars, and their new husbands who promised them all of these things. They hung over the sides of the ship, wildly waving, as the ship sauntered up to the dock, so far away from towns like Yass, Mudgee, Wagga Wagga, and Zetland. Jenny squinted; she thought she saw Ted from Chicago, but the young man she was looking at was not in a white sailor uniform, and he didn't look as handsome in a brown shirt. Waving, he held up a sign with "Jenny" painted in big black letters. She jumped up and down. "That's my Ted, girls, there he is."

Muriel was still squinting into the crowd, while my mother posed for the cameras, aware of her good looks and sure that her smile would get her in the morning newspaper, no doubt in San Francisco's society section. The gang planks were in place and the U.S. customs desks were quickly assembled. The excited young Australian women lined up to be processed and allowed in to America. Customs agents growled for them to stay in line, throwing up their hands in the air when one woman would suddenly recognize the man she had married and run out of line to kiss her waiting husband, just for a few delicious seconds. Some tried to climb over barriers, waving and shouting to men they hardly knew but had committed to a life together.

"Damn, these women don't listen. No respect for authority, even the U.S. Customs, but boy, what good-looking chicks they have in Australia,"

My mother went through the lines, showing her papers that the Red Cross had given the war brides, which would allow them speedy entrance into the U.S. Three hundred women were through those lines in forty-five minutes. Their first greeting into this land by friendly customs agents was often "Welcome to the U.S., and honey, if your husband doesn't show up, here's my number".

"My husband's over there, a petty officer in the Navy," my mother said with pride.

"You mean Frank Sinatra over there eating peanuts?" asked an agent.

Leaning on an empty luggage trolley, slowly folding the newspaper, my father sauntered over and kissed the woman he had married behind the altar in a Queensland church, promising to love, honour, cherish, and bring up the children as Catholics. Muriel from Rockhampton was still waiting for her husband; she hadn't heard from him for many months before leaving Australia, not since she wrote and told him that she was coming to join him in America and would be arriving on the *Lurline*.

"Come on, luv, he'll be here. You'll be right; probably his train is late," my mother said trying to comfort her friend.

The three of them, my mother and father and Muriel waited five hours, until the passenger wharf was empty except for a few dock workers sitting on the luggage trolleys, playing cards. My mother said she didn't care if they missed the train to Kansas; they'd take the next one. Even if they did have to wait three days, she wasn't going to leave Muriel here by herself.

"I've gotta stick by her till he comes to get her," she told Hart. "I'm not leaving her by herself here." Quietly, my father conceded; giving in was easier than trying to understand women, and he knew he was wasting his breath.

Leaving a message with the Customs Office, in case Muriel's husband eventually showed up—we all rented a room in a dingy hotel near the San Francisco wharves. Taking Muriel's papers and old letters from the man she had married a few years before in Queensland, my father—the only one familiar with American telephone procedure and anxious for the Muriel episode to be over so he could bed down with his wife—called the operator to get Muriel's husband's number. There was a listing for that name in Salt Lake City, and when a female voice answered the phone, he handed it over to Muriel. The voice at the other end said, "Sorry, Frank is at work. Could I take a message? I'm his wife." Muriel slid to the floor, sobbing, while my mother grabbed the phone yelling, "That bludger married a good Australian girl in the war, and she's here in San Francisco! If he doesn't call back in a day, we'll call the coppers and the bloody U.S. Navy! He's a bloody two-timer!"

Frank called the hotel that night; by this time, except for Muriel's occasional sobbing, everyone had calmed down and had a strategy for getting her back to her home when the ship would head down to Australia in seven days. My father said that Frank should pay for Muriel's fare back to Australia, as well as paying for the hotel. The money was sent via Western Union three days later, directly to Matson Steamship Company, and Muriel had her ticket back to Australia. My parents would wait with her so she would be safe and not alone.

If Wichita was like San Francisco, perhaps the two years wouldn't be too hard, my mother thought. She climbed the hills and explored the streets every morning with me strapped in the front of her in a canvas carrier. It reminded her of Sydney—a beautiful bridge, ferries, the ocean, and on some nights, Muriel would stay in the hotel, baby-sitting, while her two friends went to the local clubs to listen to the swing bands. Perhaps life could be bearable if she could stay in San Francisco but on her morning walks when she saw the ships resting at the docks, her chest would feel clogged with a homesick longing, almost stopping her breath. Standing by the shore, facing in a south-west direction, my mother would wave as people passed by. "I'm wavin' to Australia," she would say, in answer to their quizzical glances. "Yoo hoo, Glad, it's your mate Peggy. I am here in bloody Yankee land."

Muriel needed to go out, my mother told my father. "Take her to listen to some music, and maybe forget things for a while."

The next day, after returning from her daily walk, my mother came back to the small room and opened the door to see Muriel and my father in the same bed. Muriel said she was sorry, but at least Peggy had a husband. My father said it was my mother's fault, she had forced him to do this by refusing to sleep with him as man and wife. Muriel left, saying that she was cashing in her ticket; she liked San Francisco and was staying. After flinging every ashtray into the wall and slapping my father, my mother paid for the hotel room using most of her own money. She thought it has been a nice respectable sum, but after transferring her pounds into American dollars it was barely enough to pay for the five days in the hotel, with only a few Australian pounds left over.

"If you ever do that again to me, I will leave you," she warned.

"And just where would you go?" Hart said, laughing.

"I'd get back to Australia if I had to bloody swim with this baby on my back."

The train went through places that Peggy had only heard about in the cowboy pictures on Saturdays at the Empire picture show in Surry Hills, names like Dodge City, Laredo, and Kansas City. They looked different at the Empire picture show; the baddies got shot, and women danced in dance halls, kicking up their legs, with lots of frilly petticoats and feathers in their hair. She remembered all those times that she and Glad would get excited, pretending they were Claire Trevor kissing John Wayne after they saw the movie *Stagecoach*. Rough cowboys sliding glasses down a bar for more whiskey—they were tall, dark, hairy, and dusty. After the whiskey went down in one gulp, their big, strong hands swiped their mouths, and then they grabbed the most beautiful dance-hall girl by the arm and pulled her close. The Dodge City that Peggy saw from this train window didn't even have a pub. There was nothing about this west that looked wild. Women who were smart enough to wear petticoats and feathers in their hair would never live in the places she saw from the window of this tiny space inside a carriage of the old Santa Fe Pacific Railroad train. American pictures were all bloody lies. Chips Rafferty didn't tell lies. The "Rats of Tobruk" was a real story. She wished she had taken the screen test for *The Rats of Tobruk* and not listened to her father, who told her to stay away from that mongrel Rafferty after he approached her on Pitt Street to take a screen test, telling her that she was photogenic and could be in the pictures.

Eunice and Milton were waiting to greet them on the far end of the platform. Milton walked ahead of his wife, near the edge of the station platform, so he could see the train coming in the distance; Eunice tugged on his shirt. "Don't rush, Milton, stand back, and see what this son of yours has brought home now."

Eunice continued talking while Milton was silent, his eyes searching the station platform.

"A foreigner with a baby, and do we really know if the baby is his? These foreign women trap our boys into marriage just to get to America. Ruth's son Bill brought home a girl after the war, and she's dark and sits on the floor all day, and doesn't say anything. I think she might be a nigra from some island. Now, Bill is off with some other girl, and Ruth is left with this coloured girl, sitting legs crossed in the corner all day. What's poor Ruth going to do with her?"

"I swear, Milton, if this girl is dark and sits in the corner, I am going to Birdie's house, and I won't come back till you and that boy pack her off. And she better not go anywhere near my collection of bride dolls. What's Reverend Glass going to think? He won't stay in a house with a nigra."

Milton thought his son was playing a trick on them; the beautiful woman walking next to his boy was Gene Tierney, but how did he get a movie star to go along with this joke? Milton, still staring, hadn't acknowledged his son. My father, holding me, said, "See, Dad? I know how to do some things right."

My mother wore a cream-coloured shantung suit and high heels. Her auburn hair was piled on top of her head, and a white silk flower was tucked above her right ear. Eunice pulled away when my mother leaned towards her to kiss her cheek. On the way back to the house, Eunice sat in the back with my mother, not saying a word, but when I started to wail from the front seat, Eunice asked, "Is she hungry?"

"No, she was fed on the train," my mother answered. "God, its bloody hot and flat here."

"Isn't it hot where you come from?"

"Yes, but it doesn't make your makeup melt."

"Then don't wear any," Eunice suggested. "We dress for comfort here, not to show off."

Standing in front of the white house, looking at the rocking chairs on the veranda, my mother cried fearful that she would be rocking in those chairs forever, till she was an old woman.

"Isn't this a nice house?" my father asked. "I didn't grow up in this house, but it was right on this spot."

The original plans of my grand parent's house were bought for a dollar in the famous Sears, Roebuck Catalogue. The dollar could be used towards the lumber and building supplies, provided the customer bought them from Sears & Roebuck. So Milton and Roy tore down the old two-bedroom house and built the new one with three bedrooms and a porch.

"It's alright," my mother answered, the tears and melted Max Factor makeup starting to drip down her cheeks.

"What do you mean, alright?" Hart demanded. "It's a lot better than that hovel you lived in—no front yard, couldn't swing a cat in that hovel."

Peggy said she wished she was in that hovel now. "Only two years; one and a half left for you in the Navy, and six months to pack up and take the boat back to Sydney ... if I don't go bloody nuts first."

"OK, but we will have to stay here till we get on our feet," he said.

Grandpa Milton knocked on the bedroom door and then entered, carrying a baby crib. Embarrassed and trying to pretend he didn't see the streaks running down Peggy's cheeks, he sat next to her on the bed. "I made this in my shop for the baby," he said. "Do you know, you look just like Gene Tierney? Have you heard of her?"

My mother said yes, she had, and she told him about the Australian movie star Chips Rafferty and her own almost-movie career in *The Rats of Tobruk*. Milton said he had seen every Gene Tierney movie ever made. "I went to see her in *Laura* all by myself, the other night when Eunice was at a prayer meeting, and I thought, boy, if I was married to her I wouldn't spend much time out in my wood shop." They both laughed.

My mother liked this man, who reminded her of her father, except he spoke softer and probably would never call anyone a poofter. He moved around his house not saying much, letting Eunice do all the bossing. The pine crib was so sturdy and he said that no matter how hard she rocked it, it wouldn't tip over.

Eunice came in with a small crocheted pillow, mattress, and blanket to fit the new crib. She could see that my mother had been crying. She didn't like anyone crying in her house.

"I just told our guest the Reverend Mr. Glass—he can talk to the spirits, you see, and is staying in the next room for a while—and when I told him your father died a few years ago, he said that when we have the séance on Saturday, he will try to make contact with your father. Wouldn't that be nice? Now let's all go sit on the porch and have some nice iced tea."

Too tired to talk, my mother just smiled and thought to her self, *what the hell is a séance, and tea with ice?*

She would find out just what a séance was at exactly two o'clock the following Saturday. There was Milton and Eunice, Birdie and slow-witted Roy, my father and mother, and a lady from the Evangelical Pentecostal Community Church.

The small dining-room table was covered in a lace cloth, and the blanket covered the windows, as it had the week before, except for one little opening that threw a dancing shadow in the corner. Reverend Glass had orchestrated down to the last detail the atmosphere that he said was welcoming to the spirit world. He'd spent thirty minutes fussing and fidgeting in this tiny room before he would open the door and allow anyone to enter. Dressed in a blue suit with the same colour tie, my mother thought he looked more like a "wharfie at a funeral". He sat at the end of the table in a high-backed chair with a glass of water in front of him. He began to hum in a low tone as his guests were seated. The humming was almost inaudible, but with the waving of his arms and the rolling of his head, he beseeched forces from another plane to float into this humble dining room in America's hot, dry Midwest town.

As his head rolled clockwise and then counter-clockwise, his dishevelled blond hair mixed with the sweat of his brow. Stopping for a minute, he dropped his chin down, and his whole body seemed to go limp. Total silence took over the room for many seconds, and then he suddenly was resurrected in a sudden burst of energy, banging on the table and holding his arms up, as if another power had taken control of his whole being and was pulling him on strings like a puppet.

"There is someone here tapping me on the shoulder. Says he is a gardener. Is there anyone who has loved one in the spirit world that loved to garden?"

"Oh, yes," said the lady from the Evangelical Pentecostal Community Church. "It's my father, and I think I can see him in the corner in his gardening clothes." She waved towards the corner of the room, where the only light had been allowed to sneak in between the carefully arranged curtains.

My mother said she stared so long at that corner that she thought she actually did see something move, but then she realized there was nothing there, just some con man 'havin' them on'. When the gardener in the corner had left abruptly the reverend continued,

"Peggy, your father is here. Is there anything you want to ask him?"

"Dadda, should I stay the two years here?" Peggy asked.

"Well, darlin," you do what you think is best. These are swell people." The message came from Glass's lolling blond head.

My mother stood up, looking around the table. "You're all a bunch of bloody ratbags. If my father was going to talk to me from the grave, he wouldn't do it in a bloody American accent." Her hands were shaking as she reached in the pocket of her skirt and took out a cigarette, her brown eyes glaring at my father for some sign of support, even if it was only to reach over with a match. Instead, he walked out of the room, got into his father's car, and drove away. Reverend Glass started violently coughing from the smoke, and that was the end of the séance as the spirits would refuse to enter a room with cigarette smoke.

How long, Peggy wondered, would she have to stay here with Eunice, Milton, and the Reverend's strange talk about the spirit world? He never said "spirits"; it was always "in spirit" or "spirit world". If she had to stay in this house more than a month, she might be pulled into this life and drown. She had heard about being brainwashed by people like Mr. Glass and his talk of "spirit".

4

THE ESCAPE

Dear Glad,

I hate it here in Yankee land. When I say I am well, I mean to say that there is plenty of food here, and my mother-in–law, Eunice, means well, and the house is very clean. She always has toys for the baby and seems to at least want to hold her now. At first I think she was expecting us to be Aborigines, although she doesn't seem to know anything about Australia. No one here does. There is never any Australian news, and I still don't know who won the Melbourne Cup. I hope Hart can find a little flat for us, but he doesn't seem to try. He comes home late at night, after I have been here all day. Eunice said she would baby-sit if we wanted to go to the pictures—they call them "movies" here. She says young marrieds need to spend time together, but he didn't come home early enough, and we had a fight, right then and there in front of Eunice and Milton. Eunice started to stick up for him, but Milton gave her a look, and she shut up, and they both went out on the porch. They love to sit on porches over here, and sticky beak at the neighbours, and drink weak tea with ice in it that tastes like piss. I went to the store yesterday with Eunice. They call it a supermarket, but I don't know what's so "super" about it—no Vegemite or Billy tea.

Eunice won't let me do anything in the kitchen and seems to get nervous when I even try to heat up baby food. I can tell they don't want us here. There is a man, Mr. Glass, staying here; he's a bit of a ratbag. Says he can talk to people who have died. Ask Father O'Brien if trying to speak to the dead is a mortal sin; if he doesn't know, ask Sister Anne. I have a funny feeling about this Mr. Glass, but he stays out of my way and only nods when we see each other. Sometimes they all sit around the table and hold hands, close their eyes, and try to speak to Hart's cousin, Lionel, who was killed at Pearl Harbour.

Don't forget to find out if that's a mortal sin. I don't want to go to hell because of these ratbags. Milton goes off to the Mason meeting, and Hart says Masons don't like Catholics, so he said I shouldn't have any rosary beads hanging around.
I have no money left only a few pounds. We needed it to pay the hotel bill in San Francisco. We lived it up for a week, Glad, and I wish we had stayed in San Francisco. It reminds me of Sydney, and its closer to Sydney. Thanks for visiting Mumma every day, I know she's cranky sometimes, but I miss her and wish I was home, and we were pulling my poor Dadda off the Rosebery tram.

Your loving friend,

Peggy

Dear Mum,

We are doing so good here in America, and I just love living here. They grow corn and wheat in fields, and it is so pretty. We are looking for a little flat to rent, and then we will buy a nice house. Hart is working two jobs, and my precious little baby is getting bigger every day. We drink iced tea on the porch every night. Did you ever put ice and lemon in tea, Mumma? It tastes beautiful; don't put milk in it, though. My new mother-in-law is so nice, and she is always laughing and is teaching me to cook American food, like fried chicken and biscuits. They call scones "biscuits" here. My father-in-law is nice, too. Take care of yourself, Mumma, and maybe we can send you your fare over here soon. Give my love to everyone.

Your loving daughter,

Peggy

P.S. Every house has the phone on here, as well as a car—sometimes two cars.

Milton went off to work every day, came home, and went straight to his wood shop in the backyard. There was never any beer in the house, and when Peggy would go for walks, she couldn't even find a pub at all, let alone one with a Ladies Lounge. There were no taxis in the street, and on some streets, no footpaths, leaving her to wheel the pram on the rocky, dry roads. It was a "dry county", they told her, when she asked where to go for a beer, thinking that meant it was hot and dry, before my father explained that "dry county" meant that it was illegal to sell liquor, although his breath smelled of whisky on the nights he did come home.

Eunice would hold her breath and walk outside when her new daughter-in-law lit a cigarette, and Mr. Glass went into exaggerated coughing fits, spitting all over the tablecloth. She ignored them all. The Saturday afternoon séance continued without this Aussie swearing and causing a commotion. They said her strange language and smoking blocked the fragile crossing from the world beyond into the corner of a dining room, where no one dined, in this Sears & Roebuck house.

Eunice told her lady friends at church, "In the beginning, the good Lord knows we tried to make her feel comfortable." Eunice even took Peggy along to the quilting bees, where to the other ladies' horror and Eunice's embarrassment, she held a cigarette in one hand and the needle and thread in the other. When two hands were needed to hold the small piece of calico and stitch it to the batting, Peggy let the cigarette dangle from her mouth and squinted through the smoke in her eyes. Stitching came easy to a girl who had, for eight hours a day, bound books in a printing factory since she was fourteen, and her stitches were far neater and her fingers much more nimble than the other ladies sitting in the circle, who had learned the craft as children. The pained look on her face revealed her utter distaste for sewing, a look that said she would rather be scrubbing a dirty toilet. Peggy told Eunice that she wasn't ever going back to the quilting bee, but the ladies never invited her back anyway. They said she smoked too much and didn't like quilting or crafts; maybe it was because she was Catholic. On the second Sunday after her arrival, Eunice, along with her friend Helen, took Peggy to the revival meeting at the First Pentecostal Church. "She needs to know some good Christians and let the word of Jesus in her heart," Eunice told Helen. When relating these stories much later, my mother would tell me that the limping minister reminded her of Charlie Chaplin from the picture shows and she got a fit of the giggles when he walked like a penguin up and down the raised platform, yelling at the top of his voice, "Repent! Repent your sins and you will see the glory! Yes, my dear sinners, you will see the glory of *Jah-sus*. He will never leave you!"

Rock of Ages, cleft for me,
Let me hide myself in Thee.

The weekly séance was never quite able to make contact with Lionel or to find anyone in the spirit world who knew what Lionel was up to. They came close sometimes, just enough to get a flicker from Birdie and a smug nod from Eunice that she had done right by her sister. The Reverend would begin in a deep slow voice to say something about Lionel's Navy uniform and his boyhood toys, describing with a fake smile Lionel's blond hair and shy grin—things he had noted from visiting the boy's bedroom. After a few minutes his body would suddenly go limp, falling back on his chair with feigned exhaustion. His arms would be held out and his head would roll and hang on one side, like Christ on the cross. Cleverly and at just the right moment he would leave his benefactors to wait another week in anticipation. For both Eunice and her frail sister, it was enough to fill the next seven days with hope for a little more. After one of these sessions, my mother came face to face with the reverend in the hallway, where she had been crouched, listening.

She told him, "I know what you're doing, taking these people for a ride, you bludger. Just keeping that poor woman's hopes up that her son is alive is a mortal sin, and you'll burn in hell."

"This is no business of yours, you Catholic Jezebel," the reverend responded.

"Get away from me, you bloody ratbag poofta!"

A few weeks later, Eunice's friend Helen was walking by and opened the gate and sat with Eunice and Reverend Glass, who she believed was a visiting relative. She asked Grandma Eunice if she ever contacted the reverend from Tallahassee with the special powers. Eunice just shook her head no, remembering the warning that she was not to tell anyone about his visit, identity or purpose.

Mr. Glass didn't say a word, and Helen went on to say that in the church paper, his name was never mentioned anymore, not after that original story, and it was rumoured that he was a dishonest person taking advantage of good Christian people.

Turning to Eunice after Helen left, the very Reverend Glass asked her what she thought happened to Lionel.

"Well," Eunice said, "I know Lionel was a good boy. The bombing was around 11:15 on a Sunday morning, and he would have been in church. I think he was close to where the bombing was, probably the navy base chapel that was damaged."

Picking up the story, Mr. Glass seized his opportunity, and the next day they had their last séance. Closing his eyes, he went into staged convulsions. "I am making contact with someone in spirit world who knows what happened to Lionel. Praise the Lord, this man knows Lionel and is coming to me through spirit. He says that Lionel was not killed. He was in church, and a beam from the roof fell on his head, and he is wandering around the jungles of Hawaii. He is alive and needs me to find him."

Later that night, Milton asked the reverend to join him in his workshop to speak to him in private. He threatened to cut off the reverend's balls with his wood saw if he ever returned.

Everything was out of the small bedroom before the next morning, and they never saw him again. Milton told his wife he had given the reverend his fare to Hawaii, and the reverend's parting words were for them not to give up, as they were getting closer to finding Lionel. Birdie set an extra place at the table and would always answer the doorbell, shaking in excited anticipation for Lionel to be standing there, until she died four years later. My mother was right on one thing: Mr. Glass was a "bloody ratbag," she was never sure about him being a poofter.

The small bedroom next to ours was only empty for two weeks when Milton's deaf mother, Lucy, arrived on a bus, after riding three hundred and fifty miles from Oklahoma for her annual summer visit. If they were happy to see her, they certainly kept it to themselves. Nothing had been said about her pending arrival, and they picked her up at the bus station in town on their way home from grocery shopping, unloading her and her small, ragged suitcase in the bedroom with the same concern they showed the bag of potatoes thrown in the pantry.

Apparently, Lucy's spirit was not dampened by their lack of concern for her comfort. She immediately went into the backyard, with a bar of soap in one hand and a small bundle of blue gingham cloth in the other. Stripping off her travel clothes, she grabbed the hose and squirted off the dust and sweat from the overnight ride, dried herself by running around the yard in her wet, baggy bloomers, and jumped in the air, delighting herself with the near-naked freedom. She then pulled the blue-checked cotton dress over her head, running her fingers through her stringy grey hair. Going back into the house, she took a small black bag from her suitcase and then went out on to the porch, sat in a rocker, and chewed on the small bundle while the brown juices from tobacco trickled down the corners of her thin lips. She eventually rocked herself to sleep and snored loudly. In an effort to drown out the noise, Eunice talked louder, especially when people were strolling by. She explained to my mother that Lucy came every year that Milton and his brothers took turns in having their mother visit.

"She's family, and there's nothing more important than family, you know."

Despite this declaration of blood alliance, Eunice ignored her mother-in-law, except to watch and count every piece of bread she ate and to exclude her from her two weekly excursions, the Piggy Wiggly supermarket and Sunday church. What would the people from her church say if they knew she had a woman in her house twice a year who chewed tobacco and wasn't sure who Milton's father was, or his brother Bill's father, or his other brother Jim's father?

The only time Milton raised his voice to Eunice was when she called his mother "a hillbilly whore". Milton told his wife that if she ever said that again or called his mother names, he would do something he had never done before and give her "a whoopin'". He told her that his mother was a good woman who had raised her three law-abiding boys alone, with no help from anyone. In spite of her affliction Lucy imparted a loving sense of security and happiness through the years they were growing up. They were unaware of their poverty as there was no one around to tell them so. There was always plenty of squirrel stew, possum, and greens from her yard. His mother laid traps for the rabbits going out every morning, hardly ever coming home with nothing to eat for her boys, even in winter, he said.

Once when they were young boys, Milton reminisced, she came home with a pheasant. She had wrapped herself in corn stalks and stood still and straight in a field for hours, and then pounced, like a flash of lightening, grabbing the pheasant by the legs when it started to fly and quickly twisting its neck as if wringing out the wash. She cooked it with berry juice. "That bird was better than anything you ever cooked, Eunice."

While Milton wouldn't hear of any criticism of his mother, he continued to come home from the factory, go into his workshop in the back of the house, and not come in until dinner time. He never talked to his mother, other than an occasional sad glance at this little, stooped woman. Every year he noticed that she had less hair and was a little more bent over. He wondered how he could have felt so safe as a young boy. His survival, as well as his two brothers' survival, had been dependant on this tiny woman.

He remembered that she had always been barefoot, her wheat-coloured hair tied back with twine as she darted from one chore to the next—digging in the garden, rubbing their ragged clothes back and forth on a washboard—always making her own distinct happy sounds as if humming to herself. Occasionally, she would take in a visitor for the day, and they would be sent outside to play. Usually, they got a new pair of pants and shoes soon after.

Lucy's feet never seemed to touch the ground. Her thin body glided silently over the floor, and this gave her a delighted edge. She would follow people, scaring them as they turned around, aghast, only a few inches from her wrinkled, toothless grin. It was a game she played everywhere, and she discriminated against no one, whether in the street to strangers or in the house to family, she found it increasingly amusing. She would wait around corners and appear like an apparition, a scary, old, unpredictable woman with a face like Popeye the Sailor Man, who wrung the neck of birds.

After a few weeks of Lucy's crazy antics, my mother who slept with the door locked and furniture up against the door, decided she was going to teach the old Okie a lesson. One morning in the kitchen, my mother suspected the old girl was waiting in the hallway to jump out at her as she had for the last several days. Slipping out the front door, Peggy crawled silently around to the back of the house, away from view, where she picked up her hidden, waiting costume. With a sheet over her head, eyes already cut out; she put on a black cowboy hat and my father's Navy goggles, and then quietly crept up behind Lucy, who was patiently waiting for my mother to turn the corner in front of her. With a gentle tap on the shoulder, Lucy turned around, laughing with delight that she had found someone to share her favourite game, but within seconds she began coughing and choking. As the breathing and gasping became wheezy, my mother panicked and punched her in the back, dislodging the juicy, brown wad from her mouth, leaving both of them lying on the floor, exhausted, and my mother, frightened that she might have killed this tough old bird. Eunice, hearing the commotion, ran in from the yard to see her new daughter-in-law tied up in a sheet and wearing a cowboy hat and goggles. Her bruised but grinning mother-in-law was leaning against the wall, and on the broadloom between the two of them was a big wad of juicy chewed-up tobacco.

Peggy was never embarrassed by Lucy's games of jumping at strangers from behind corners, and the two women went for walks every day, pushing me in the pram, while Eunice stayed behind, waving them on with her hand. "I have work to do. I don't have time to walk around the streets."

It was August; the brown grass and droopy flowers behind the picket fences were bowing out not so gracefully to this hot, dry world. The dusty red strip of earth between the paved roads and the buildings waited for the excitement of whirlwinds to pick it up and dance. Most of the houses they passed had porches like Milton and Eunice's, with a path leading to the front door and more land around them. A waste of space, Peggy thought, not like the only two homes she had known in Sydney—out of the door three steps and you were right there on a footpath. They ventured a little farther every day, sometimes as far as the railroad tracks, and ignored Eunice's warnings of "I won't have anyone in my house going down there, all white trash and nigras". Curious, and drawn by the shouting of children and the sharp, bitter odour of chemicals coming from the factories, they stopped in the City Café, a small wooden shack squeezed between two factories, Worthington Press and Wright's Mill. A young Negro man came out with two wooden chairs when he saw both women trying to squeeze the pram inside the door. "Hey, ladies, sit out here, and I'll bring you a drink. How about a nice cold sarsaparilla?"

"Wonder if they have book binders in that printing factory." Thinking out loud, Peggy continued talking as though Lucy could hear; it didn't matter, she just talked. "You know, Lucy, I could have been a movie star. Chips Rafferty wanted me to take a screen test." Lucy nodded, then pulled out her black purse with the zipper and took a hunk of tobacco, swirling it around with the sarsaparilla in her swollen cheek.

The daily visits to the City Café made the long, hot, August Kansas days bearable for both of them. The young man would laugh when Lucy suddenly appeared behind his kitchen door, a toothless, grinning vision. My mother told him that Lucy was harmless, and he said, "No mind. I love old crazy women."

Evenings, the whole family sat on the porch, except for my father, who didn't come home much. Eunice would talk about the church and the good works that she did. Her sister, Birdie, hadn't received word from Hawaii, but she was sure the reverend was in the jungle, searching. Milton said nothing; he just read the paper. My mother's mind would be back in Sydney, thinking of the times her father would take her down to the city to see the bridge. On the special days, they would climb the many stairs up the dark centre of the cement pylon and be rewarded with the spectacular view of blue water and tiny sailboats weaving around the busy harbour ferries. What was her friend Gladys doing right now? She pictured her mum, snipping at the roses. And she thought of the fun she'd had with the girls from the *Sun* at the Troc. She missed it all so much that it was a physical pain that hurt right in the middle of her chest. She would have to put her hand firmly against her chest to stop it from breaking through her skin and falling out on the floor, throbbing from homesickness. Lucy watched the tears fall down Peggy's face and opened her tobacco purse, pulling out thin, white papers and rolling tobacco between her palms in a perfect cylinder. She lit it and handed it over to her with a wink. Eunice shuddered in disgust, while Milton kept reading his paper.

After a month, they put Lucy on the bus back to Oklahoma. At my mother's insistence, she rode along to say good-bye, wedged between the old, ragged suitcase and a bag of corn on the cob, a going-away present, still wrapped in its husk. Eunice didn't kiss this little woman good-bye, and Milton just patted her on the shoulder. But in the month that Lucy lived in the house on Magnolia Drive with this young Aussie, the bride of the grandson she had seen only twice in the past month, they had found a way to communicate, discovering a kinship of common humour. They both made fun of poor Eunice behind her back, with Lucy patting herself on the rear when her daughter-in-law would scold her about her tobacco. It didn't matter whether the word was "asshole" or "arsehole"; they giggled, understanding the silent gesture.

When Lucy came into our room, she would pick up the pictures of my Australian grandmother, a shot of Peggy and Gladys taken by a wandering photographer walking around Martin Place, and a picture of my grandfather and Mick in the ANZAC Day parade. She pointed to me, then the pictures, and pulled out my mother's suitcase, patting her on the cheek, her eyes warning Peggy to go home.

Hugging my mother at the bus stop, she screwed up her face at me, which I am told always made me laugh. Then she walked a few steps and turned around, taking one ear of corn out of the bag. She pointed it out under her belly, its limp, silk tassel hanging like a spent phallus. She winked at my mother and turned around, her skinny legs springing her body up the bus steps, back to her beloved shack somewhere in Oklahoma.

The days were long without Lucy's company and her hallway antics. Even the despicable reverend, with his fake weekly séances, would have been better than the daily routine in this empty house. Birdie came over every day for coffee, and both sisters gossiped about the sinners living around them.

Mum said she would like to meet those sinners; that it would make the next two years go faster than this bloody boring place. She lit up a cigarette, and Eunice said she wasn't a good Christian girl, what with all that smoking and strange language and she had no business being disrespectful to Mr. Glass when he was there. Eunice was sure she wouldn't have called a Roman Catholic priest a poofter, even though she didn't know the meaning of the word (it just sounded worse than ratbag and bludger, the other names she had heard Peggy call him to his face). Milton went to his wood shop every night after dinner, and on the few nights my father did come home, they would argue, and he would leave my mother sobbing, knowing that it would probably be days before she would see him again.

"Take the bloody bus or walk home," she would tell him when he said the reason he didn't come home often was because he didn't have a car and had to rely on someone to give him a lift.

"I have to have money to buy a car; a man can't get by without a car. That's why I stay in town with a friend. Where is the money I gave you?"

"That's for our trip back to Sydney, and you're not getting it."

Peggy would put up with living in this house with Eunice if it allowed them to save his pay checks, but he had stopped giving her his pay checks a while back, and they were certainly a long way from having enough to buy a car or to get back to Australia. From her calculations, they had just enough for the train ride back to San Francisco.

Two days later, when he did return, he found my mother packing up the suitcase, taking her beloved photos, a little blue statue of the Blessed Virgin, and a small wooden Buddha, looking so happy with his hands sticking up to heavens, Hart's gift to her from the Philippines. Maybe this was all she needed for luck. She looked at the crib and decided that I would have to sleep in the pram. She thought there were worse things than sleeping in a pram; maybe she could get the crib later. She told my father that they were moving to a flat on the other side of town, on Sycamore Street.

"That is nigger town, and I'm not moving there," he told her.

"Well, living here is like a bloody jail, and I'm not staying here one more day." He was gone for days, and she wasn't saving any money anyway.

He sat on the bed, pushing his hair back, and she felt sorry for him. "Aw come on, luv," she coaxed. "We can do it. It'll be real nice, just the three of us. It's not fair to be bludging off your mother and father. And Mrs. Merry said I can use her pots and pans if I want to cook, and she has an old couch she can give us."

Everything was happening so fast that his head was spinning. Who the hell was Mrs. Merry?

That morning my mother had gotten out of bed, with no husband beside her—hadn't been there all night. She got dressed and decided then to change her life in this here United States of America. "Land of the free, home of the bloody brave." She walked out of the house on Magnolia Street towards the City Café, passing it and waving to the young man sweeping the sidewalk, the young man who loved old crazy women.

"Don't work too hard, Billy," she yelled as she pushed the pram over the holes in the road. As she pushed the pram faster, the fear and dread of being trapped with her in-laws forever gave her energy to keep on going. The anger was slowly being walked out of her, and she slowed down and the relief came over her. Suddenly, she realized she had no idea of her destination. She walked over railroad tracks and down past the Piggly Wiggly. *What a stupid bloody name for a grocery store*, she thought. Why hadn't she come down here before? No one told her these nice shops were here, each one getting smarter than the next, with painted wood mannequins wrapped in fur coats that glistened and high-heeled boots, the tops trimmed with fur to match. Even wood mannequins looked haughty in fur, head high in the air with their smug painted faces. She looked down at her plain brown skirt and realized her cream silk blouse had wet armpits, the sweat from the heat and excitement of her decision to escape.

September was considered autumn, but in Kansas it was hot. Winter would come, and she hoped to see snow; maybe she could buy a fur coat. She shook her head to get that thought away from her; they needed all the money to get back to home, and nothing was going to tempt her away from that. Past the nice shops she kept walking, to the other side of the city, not turning any corners so that she could find her way back if she couldn't find a flat to rent or a boarding house nearby. The street started to change; there were a few small factories, with workers hanging outside who whistled as she passed. Smiling, she walked, swinging her hips with each step. It felt so good to flirt again. On either side of the first brick factory was a small house, each with peaked roofs and peeling paint. The front doors topped the back edge of the steaming concrete sidewalk. No room for a garden, but the residents didn't seem to mind. The music coming from inside sounded like a band; anyone who played that music was happy and didn't worry about a garden. They probably liked stepping right out of their front door on to the crowded sidewalk.

She came across another square, dark brown concrete building; its doors open for a breeze and men shouting above the buzzing machines. After months on Magnolia Street, sitting on the porch with iced tea and disapproving looks from Eunice when she lit a cigarette, she wanted to be part of this street, with factories buzzing like the bindery at the Sun office, and music and laughter behind doors. Less than a year ago, she was part of a lively town, and there was always somewhere to go. Her sturdy mother, who never smiled, went about taking care of her and her baby. Thinking about her mother, Peggy vowed that when she got home, she would treat her better and not get mad at the things she said about her father. (If he loved her so much, and he knew how proud she was, then why did he drink and let people see him with wet pants, sleeping in the gutter?) Had her mother had the same hopes about being married, picturing it one way and it ending up another? *Here I am in bloody Kansas, with a husband I barely see, who promised to love, honour, and obey*, she though. Yes, she decided, walking through that hot day in a rundown Wichita neighbourhood, her thoughts suddenly returning to the mother who had adopted her as an infant. When she got home she would peel the potatoes closer to the skin, buy Maude flowers, and take her to lunch over to Manly on the ferry as often as she could. The Manly ferry—oh, what she would give to be sitting on its upper deck, rocking when it went through the intense waves by the ocean heads. The pain in her chest started stabbing at her again. Sitting down in the gutter, she took her baby out of the hot pram. This would be as good a time as any, with all these mixed up thoughts, running through her head …

Hail Mary, full of grace,
The Lord is with thee,
Blessed art thou among women …

"Honey child, you must be lost. Is you lost?"

The woman wasn't the vision draped in blue that appeared in Lourdes, Fatima, or wherever else; she was a wide lady of colour, looming over us, her big breasts straining the buttons of her red dress. The four little boys, two on each side of her, clung to her skirt and frowned at these two strangers sitting in the gutter.

"No, luv, I can find my way home. I didn't make any turns; just came straight up the street from way down there. We crossed the train tracks."

"You sure did cross the tracks, darlin', you should not be walking so far in this heat with a baby." With that, she ordered my mother to take off all my clothes. "All that baby needs is a something to cover her bottom. What are you thinking, crazy young girl?" She shook her head.

Mum told her exactly what she was thinking. She shared the thoughts in her head about her mother and that she couldn't take another day living with Eunice, Milton, and the whole bloody crazy bunch of ratbags, or the husband who never came home. Despite the jumbled-up litany of her life tumbling out in tearful incoherency, this lady listened thoughtfully, and within a few minutes our life had a plan. We followed her through one of the doors on the edge of the sidewalk, her skirt dragging the four little boys who were scared to let go and be alone with a crying white woman and her whiter half-naked baby.

It was a long, narrow house, bedrooms on each side of a hallway, and ended in a larger room that served as a kitchen and everything else. A large, scrubbed wooden table, with a black tattered Bible as its centrepiece, was flanked by four sturdy but old wooden chairs. A child's crib's was placed against one inside wall, opposite an upright piano topped with black-and-white framed snapshots. One picture was of a young man in uniform; the other was a young girl dressed in a starched white dress, a large white bow in her hair. None of them was smiling; they looked as if they had posed on the orders of someone they didn't like and were in a hurry to get the picture-taking episode over.

This big clean room smelled like vanilla. When the boys started playing, our new patron saint, the lady who had appeared to us while my mother recited her daily Hail Mary, went to another room, bought out a jug, and, taking two glass jars from a cupboard, poured out a few sips of brownish-coloured liquid.

"Here, darlin', this will make you feel better."

It burned all the way down, exploding at the pit of Peggy's stomach, sending hot, thick juice to her every nerve ending from head to toe. "I'd like another one, please."

"No, baby, you got too far to walk back. Now let's see … do

you have any money? A woman should always have a little money without anyone knowing where it is."

"Not anyone? Even my husband?"

"Girl, are you silly. Never, never tell your man if you have money."

"I have a little in my jewellery box. We're saving up to go back to my home, but while we are waiting, I want to live around here. Any flats or even rooms? I think I'll be in the bloody nut house if I stay there any longer, and Hart doesn't come home; says it's too far and he has no car. This is closer, and he'll come home, and it can be just like it was when there was only the two of us, near the Navy base in Queensland."

We always called her "Mrs. Merry", but I don't know why. Her real name was Mary Alice Pritchard. I can only guess that when she introduced herself outside her house that day as Miss Mary, my mother thought she said Mrs. Merry. But she hadn't, and even though we knew that, she was always Mrs. Merry to us. Her husband, she said proudly, was a light Negro man. He had gone up north years ago to find work and never came back. "Probably got hanged between Kansas and Virginia, where he was heading for work in the tobacco fields." She said in a manner of acceptance.

Mrs. Merry had no children of her own, but life was not lonely, she said. She took in young babies that were sometimes just left at her door, right on the street. People she knew and some she had never seen before would ask her to watch their babies for a short time and would never come back for them. Most of the time, there would just be a knock on the door, and there they would be, "at my feets, like Moses in the bulrushes". Now, she was sixty-one and had only four boys. None had been dropped off lately, and if they were, she would have to write to the welfare or the Children's Home near Topeka. "I'm getting old and tired. It's just for the best." She would say proudly, "All my childrens are good childrens. Grown up to be righteous people."

Mrs. Merry marched us around the corner, my mother pushing me in the pram, the four boys, their shyness gone; now sitting on the edges of the pram, two on each side, for the ride.

That afternoon we rented a room in the back of Mrs. Merry's friend Esther's house. Esther said she didn't have enough furniture for the empty room anyway. A white porcelain sink hung from a wall, with a mirror hanging by a nail above it and pipes twisted underneath. The walls were scrubbed to the bare wood. Peggy looked out the back window and saw the endearing vision of the backyard 'dunny' and immediately pulled ten dollars out from inside her blouse and handed it to Esther, telling her that her husband would be paying the rent from then on. Sadly, the backyard dunny proved to be just a shell from a previous era; it now contained rusty shovels and rakes. We would share the indoor toilet with Esther and her boyfriend, Rudy.

Peggy woke the next morning, still buoyed by the strength of her two new friends, Mrs. Merry and Esther. And despite the argument with my father, who left her alone, she got up early, excited that she would be living with noise and music and women who seemed to be able to take care of anything that came along with a no-nonsense sense of humour.

Eunice glanced at the address left on the dining room table and asked Peggy how she could not care about her poor baby and husband, moving them into a nigra's house.

"Just give your son this address and tell him to bring the rest of his clothes." Mum told her that in the past six months, Eunice had never cared about us, just about the mess we made in her house. Her precious son didn't come home to his wife and baby every night, and she was left there in the room, alone. And, she added, "What are you saying about the coloured? You call them nigras, you don't want to say niggers, because that might not be Christian, and you don't say Negro because that might be just a tiny bit more respect. So go to your bloody church and when you die and go to heaven, I hope the "nigras" are at the gate and spit at you, you bloody hypocrite."

There would be no going back, ever, to Eunice and Milton's after that. Milton had offered to give us a ride, but his wife's glare changed his mind, and he walked away. We left the house on Magnolia Drive, my mother furiously pushing the baby buggy, with me plopped in the middle of bundles of clothes, a mother of pearl jewellery box (a treasured birthday gift from her father), a few pictures, and a blue statue of the Virgin Mary on top of a very happy Buddha.

The rented room had been cleaned again since she had seen it the day before and Esther had added some furniture for her new friend—a wooden table and two chairs. She would buy a bed and maybe some pretty curtains that afternoon. Maybe she could spend a little of her money, and he would see how nice it was. It was closer to the recruiting office, where he was finishing out his time in the Navy, so he might come home every night. With still a year and half left before her husband could get out of the Navy, this would be home till then, and she could be so much happier here. Once they were alone, they would have a chance to be close again and not fight all the time. She would take a few dollars out of her jewellery box and go to the shops, just to get a few things. He would see how nice it was to be together as a family, without the disgusted glares from Eunice every time she lit a cigarette.

But when she opened her jewellery box, her whole body stopped still for that one moment, until her heart started throbbing with a deafening drumbeat. Tipping the box upside-down, she shook it, and only a few earrings fell out. There was no money in the box. She searched the pram, but the dollars she had saved from the only two pay checks her husband had given her along with the pounds that hadn't been changed into American money weren't there. Shillings saved from the days living with her mother, who always made her put "something away for a rainy day"—gone. The box had been under the clothes, so she hadn't dropped it on the way. She fell down on her knees and sobbed, her body wrenching with pent up emotions of despair and hopeless frustration. She vomited hard forcing herself to purge her body of these feelings, knowing that she could only think of what to do when her mind and body was cleansed to make room for her faith in God and herself.

"Well, Mumma, now I don't even have anything left for a bloody sunny day, let alone a rainy day."

Standing on the floor in the midst of her vomit, she began to pray.

Hail Mary, full of grace,
The Lord is with Thee.

She could hear Esther singing in the front of the house, but she wouldn't bother her. *These women here have had more problems in one day than I would ever know*, she thought. Mrs Merry, raising all those kids just dumped on her doorstep, and although she didn't know Esther's story, her sad eyes didn't match her perpetual smile.

With no rags or soap to clean the floor or even herself, she quickly pulled down her underpants and ran them under the tap. Then she wrung them out and, starting at the top of her head, wiped herself from head to toe, under the arms, between her legs, and then her toes. Wiping up the floor, she then threw the pants into a corner of the small room, took some biscuits out of the bottom of the pram, and we had our first meal in our new home. She pulled out a brown skirt and cream silk blouse and changed clothes. Teetering on a chair, she could see herself in the small mirror above the sink. The skirt didn't look too wrinkled, and she hoped her face might be a distraction from her crumpled blouse.

Remembering that she saw a printing factory on the other side of the city when she and Lucy had gone to lunch, she left me with Mrs. Merry. She walked fast, always refreshed by a good cry, and her determination was fuelled by her anger as she flew by the department store with its fur coats.

I'll show them. Don't piss off an Aussie girl, you bludgers, she thought, although she was not sure just where to lay the blame for her stolen money. Perhaps Reverend Glass had been snooping around or ... no, it couldn't be Hart. He wouldn't do that, although he had been telling her how much he needed a car.

Life would be better if she got a job, and she couldn't think of anyone better than Mrs. Merry, who had agreed, to watch her baby girl.

Without underpants, she walked into the printing office, determined not to leave without a job. She told the man in charge that she was a good worker. She could carry heavy bundles, had worked in the bindery for a newspaper in Sydney, and knew how to fold and collate. She added that there was another printing company across town who wanted her, but this place was closer to her home. She was hired and started the next day. Mrs. Merry added one more charge to her brood—a white kid with red hair.

That night Milton came to visit while Eunice was in church. He didn't say much, but he brought the rest of our clothes, food, and cast-off furniture that Eunice had in the garage. He was sorry that things worked out the way they did. "Eunice isn't that bad, and the burden of her sister weighs heavily on her," he said.

Mum said that that it's hard for two women to live together. "I have a hard time with my own mother sometimes, and I hope Eunice forgives me for saying those things about the nigras spitting at her, but ... well, no, don't apologize for me. She deserves it." She thought again of the horrible things that had been said between both of them on the day she left in a huff.

"It wasn't right that we were living with you. I just hope, Milton, that when Hart comes home here, we can visit one another and get along."

Milton said that Mum should try to forget my father. "He is my son but he has problems beyond anyone's help," he said.

Mum said that wars did horrible things to people. Her own father was always drunk, and now her husband couldn't settle down in marriage. "It's wars, Milton," she said.

He just shrugged, kissed us, and left.

5

THE TONI TWINS

My mother said I spent the days happily with Mrs. Merry and Benny, Willie, Teddy, and Thomas, her four little boys. I didn't want to leave at night and screamed when I had to go. At first the boys were scared to touch me, poking and pulling away at my red hair, thinking it would burn their fingers. They treated me gently, sharing every little home-made toy, and the four of them picking me up when I fell. Mrs. Merry called me Princess. When I cried, she would sing to me, and I would stop crying, feeling so safe with my head nestled into her big, warm, vanilla-smelling bosom.

"Mam," Benny would say to Mrs. Merry, "Princess pooped."

"Mam," Willie would say to Mrs. Merry, "Printheth ith being bad."

Every day before our nap, we children all got into a galvanized tub in the middle of the big room and took a bath together. The chore of heating and carrying water from a wood stove was not going to be repeated five times for the sake of segregated gender modesty. When we came out of the bath, the boys would get "greased up" in a Vaseline jelly stuff she kept in jars. She would rub it over their little bodies and hair. Sitting on a chair, a big jar of gooey grease in her hand, she'd say, "Come on, boys; get your ashen selves over here."

"Mam, Princess is crying. She wants to be greezed up too."

My mother said that she picked up a slippery baby that night.

Mrs. Merry made me my first doll. It was made out of rags, its face, legs, and arms a floral calico, and with black buttons for eyes and red wool for hair.

We would take walks in the afternoon, this gloriously large woman whose size was matched only by her big, kind heart. This lady, who appeared to us in answer to a prayer to the Mother of God, would waddle down the street, pushing a pram, two little boys sitting on each side with a lucky Princess in the middle.

My father didn't come to our one room home for quite some time, and after a few weeks, lonely and swallowing her pride, Mum called the recruiting office. They always said that he was "out in the field".

Dear Glad,

Thought I'd drop a line tonight. It's pretty lonely. I moved out of my in-laws' house and have a room at the back of my new friend Esther's place. She rents the bottom part of this house, but these rooms are not being used, and she said the landlord won't mind. Esther is a beautiful Negro girl. She is so classy; she wears fresh gardenias in her hair and walks like she always has a book balanced on her head, like when we used to practice deportment. Remember?. In the backyard with Cocky screeching. By the way, how is Cocky? It was nice of you to take him. When I get home, we'll take him to the bush, open his cage, and maybe he will fly away free. But then, he has been fed for years; he might starve if he has to find his own food. I feel very lucky to have Esther and Mrs. Merry as friends, and I don't worry about leaving my baby. You wouldn't believe it; I was so depressed and then just as I was saying a Hail Mary in the gutter, this woman was right in front of me when I opened my eyes. She is a smart woman, makes a drink from corn, and gave me the gumption to leave Eunice's and get a job. I'll make you Mrs. Merry's drink when I get home. We'll get pissed on corn liquor, if we can find corn growing in Sydney.

Diana is very happy to stay with her while I go to work. The women at the bindery are nice. Some of them have been married three times, and most of them at least twice. Maybe that's not such a bad idea. Don't wait around and waste your life. Hart is another matter; don't know if he's coming back. The war does funny things, I guess.

How is Mumma doing? I miss the old girl, but most of all, I miss home. So much to tell you, but I'm tired; was on my feet all day. Will get this in the post tomorrow.

Love,

Peggy

Esther had a boyfriend, Rudy, who came around every night. Rudy dressed like a movie star in silk suits, shoes polished like glass, and a diamond ring on his pinkie finger, and he always had a present and gardenias for Esther. Mrs. Merry said to watch out for Rudy; that he got mixed up with the wrong kind, big gangster men, and would be laughing with you while he's robbing you. My mother told Mrs. Merry that she didn't care what Rudy did; he always treated her good. Besides, there was nothing left to rob.

Defying anyone to question the legitimacy of her man's occupation, Esther, with her hands on her hips and throwing her head up, proudly declared, "My Rudy is a smart business man."

Mum said she didn't care if he was Jack the Ripper; he was better than her husband, and Esther shouldn't care what people say, but it was better that she not know what he did. "Don't ask questions, Esther, as long as he's good to you. Don't ask questions. Look at the bludger I married; doesn't come to see if we are dead or alive."

Every night after work, while walking down the narrow hallway on her way to the back room, my mother could tell if Rudy was home with Esther. She would quietly tiptoe past the closed bedroom door, and the plates on the wall shelf would dance, and the passion in the moans forced her to remember, unwillingly, a favoured part of her short marriage. She missed having a man hold her, missed feeling the charged power they had over each other. She wouldn't let herself think about it, as the lonely night ahead stretched before her. How many times could she clean one room, and feed and bathe a toddler? Perhaps she could write some letters. No, she was too tired; it was too much effort to lie again to her mother, to tell her how everything was so just so wonderful in her life. Her mind couldn't go to that place of pretended happiness, and her mother was not so simple that she wouldn't eventually read between the lines. She would see the clues in her daughter's letters. Avoiding giving those clues was hard work, and Peggy was tired tonight, too tired to write a lying, clever letter, especially since it would be followed by the sick feeling of self-loathing. Faking a life of wedded, middle-class American bliss was becoming tiring. *You're a fake,* she would tell herself. Was it because she thought that her mother would say "I told you so"? No, it was because her mother *wouldn't* say "Come on home and we'll handle this". No, she was scared to be reminded of her duty. "Do the right thing; you've made your bed with Slick. Now lie in it." No, tonight she was definitely too tired to think about it, and so she spent another night alone, thousands of miles away from the country that had so cruelly kept her heart when she sailed away.

Hail Mary full of grace,
The Lord is with Thee.
Blessed art thou among women.

Esther would wait for us to come home on the nights when Rudy was working late. She would be waiting outside on the one concrete step in front of the green door with its peeling paint. Her shapely, long, black bare legs were spread in front of her, and she was wickedly amused by the people passing by on this narrow path, forcing them to pick up their feet. Tired from a day at work in the printing factory, my mother could always be cheered with Esther's stories. Even the serious ones brought my mother to fits of laughter.

"So I said to him," Esther said about the grocer down the street, "this fruit is so rotten, I wouldn't feed it to my pigs."

"You don't have any pigs."

"Some day I'll have pigs," she answered in a huff.

"Esther," my mother asked, "what would you, a beautiful city girl, ever do with pigs?"

"Don't know, but I wouldn't feed them his rotten vegetables." And they would both fall into fits of laughter.

Esther had her own prejudice, and it had to do with the degree of darkness in her own race. She proudly referred to her father by saying that "he was a light coloured man". Of the man who lived next door, though, she said, "He's so black that at night, if he closed his eyes, you couldn't see the nigger."

"Esther, don't say that",

"I can say that but you can't"

"Well don't think just because I am white that we were not poor" Mum would tell her new friend, "We ate boiled tough meat and sometimes our dinner would be a fried egg or one potato"

When they would try to compete over which one of them was the poorest growing up, Esther would just have to say

"My mother did ironing and wash for people and we were so poor and hungry I would eat the chunks of laundry starch"

My mother never could top this, but she thought hard.

As I was growing up whenever I would complain about the food put in front of me, she would pounce on that opportunity to tell me about Esther and the starch.

On Saturdays, Esther, who always had a promise of a night out with Rudy, would walk back to our room, and she and my mother would have what they called "Hollywood Days". Esther would spend hours straightening her hair, while my mother would do everything she could to make her poker-straight hair curly. Esther would pull, drag, and twist her hair through small sections of rags, while her friend would twist small clumps of hair, then pin them tight to her head and cover it with a scarf. At that time, a miracle for all straight-haired women came on the scene: the permanent wave.

"Hey, Esther, I can have permanent curls now. We can be the bloody Toni twins." They danced around the room in the back of the little rundown house in the ghetto of Wichita, arm in arm, kicking up their lily-white and chocolate-brown legs.

T-O-N-I
It's trouble free, and odour free
and frizz free, as a wave can be,
That's how you spell a T-O-N-I for me

On one of their Hollywood Days, after a few glasses of Mrs. Merry's corn liquor, time got away from them, and they left the perm curlers in my mother's hair too long. Catching her breath in horror, Esther then screamed with uncontrollable laughter as her friend took out each one of the little curlers, which looked like tiny dog bones, and her hair stuck up in random, frizzy clumps, all over her head.

"Peggy, girl you got nappy hair."

Rudy would take Esther to the local jazz clubs on Saturday nights; their favourite was the Forum, a black club that allowed whites to sit in the balcony. That night, they saw Lionel Hampton. Esther always talked about someday going to the Cotton Club in Harlem to see her favourite singer, Billie Holiday.

"Come on, Esther, sing 'God Bless the Child'," my mother would beg.

"Why? You always start crying, you silly girl with nappy hair."

"Sometimes a good cry is good, and I don't give a bugga about my hair. Where the bloody hell do I go? Only the bindery; I'll wear a bloody scarf."

Papa may have and Momma may have,
God Bless the child that's got his own,
That's got his own.

Seeing Lena Horne in the movie *Stormy Weather* was the only association my mother had with a black singer, but she loved the way those songs and the music made her feel; she had heard it called blues or jazz. She didn't know the difference, but Rudy and Esther gave her a morsel, instilling a love for this pure music with its strangely welcome gift of soulful melancholia.

When Rudy was around, Esther shook her rear end a little more than when he wasn't, sang her Billie Holiday songs around the house, and always smelled like a gardenia.

"You know, Esther, the bloody queen doesn't dress as good as you, and she has all the money bludged off the Empire."

Esther had given up asking what some words meant; she had learned that a "bludger" was someone who lived off someone else. Although a poofta was a homosexual and was offensive, Esther learned it was a label that really encompassed anyone my mother chose to insult.

"You know, Esther, we're a couple of good sorts. I bet if Chips Rafferty—he's an Australian film star, you know—saw us, he'd put us in a picture. Did I tell you he wanted me to take a screen test for *The Rats of Tobruk?*"

"Only twenty thousand times."

Two months passed. From Monday to Friday, the routine was the same. I would be dropped off in the safe circle of Mrs. Merry and her boys. At the end of the day, my exhausted mother would pick me up, have a drink of the corn liquor that was always waiting on the table for her, and we would go back to the room she called home. The precious Saturdays were spent with Esther, who now, thanks to Rudy's business success, was the proud owner of a phonograph machine, two Billie Holiday records, one Bessie Smith, and one Frank Sinatra. Esther didn't like Frank Sinatra so she gave that record to my mother.

"He's a crooner, Esther," my mother told her, trying to show off that she knew at least something about popular American music.

"Hmmph" was all Esther thought about "crooning".

Sundays were the hardest, longest days for my mother, alone except for the company of a three-year-old. Sitting in a room that could be cleaned from top to bottom in twenty minutes, and the blue cotton printing-factory uniforms could be washed and pressed in another hour. That would leave ten hours to fill for the rest of the day and night. She would take out the box with the mother-of-pearl lid and count the money, over and over, that she had began to save again for her return to her beloved city, hoping for a miracle with every count, praying her Hail Mary's would be heard and that Mary would ask her son, Jesus, to multiply the money in this little box.

> *Dear Precious Mother of God, I know your son, Jesus, listens to you first, before any of us. Remember that time; I think it was near some sea, when your son, our dear Lord, fed many*

thousands with just a few loaves and fishes? Could you please kindly ask Him to turn my few dollars into a bit more? Not thousands, just enough to get me back home, and I'll take it from there. I'll work hard, go to Mass every Sunday, never do impure actions again, and try not to swear. I promise … with all my heart.

"Child, who are you talking to? There's no one here." Mrs. Merry stood at the doorway, holding a dish.

"How come every time I pray out loud, I open up my eyes and there you are? I was praying for money."

"Well, baby, you're going to have to be content with sweet potato pie, 'cause that's all I got for you." Our beloved benefactor said as she marched towards the cupboard.

"That was my second choice."

"The Lord just doesn't give us everything we ask for. What would be the good in that? You got the strength and health to work for your money, and you'll be so strong for all the hard times ahead."

"I'm sick of hard times; it's going to take me four years to save enough for my fare home."

"Baby, you don't know what hard times are. Eat some pie," she ordered shoving a plate and fork in my mother's hands.

My mother gave Mrs. Merry a box of four white Irish linen handkerchiefs that day; she had brought them with her from Australia, an intended gift for her new mother-in-law, but she'd never gotten around to giving them to her. The handkerchiefs were not wasted on this lovely, big, brown angel; she wore two at a time, one in her dress pocket and one tucked between her breasts, always with the embroidered "Pure Irish Linen" corner folded on the outside for everyone to see.

"You start smiling again and being grateful to the Lord for what you have: a healthy baby and good looks, although that ain't so much. There's been more tears run down a pretty face than a homely one. Tomorrow, when you come to pick up Princess, you stay for supper. I am having chitlins; you're the only white girl I know who likes chitlins."

"I'm probably the only white girl who was ever brave enough to try them. My mother is a horrible cook. She is Scottish, you know, but we had sheep brains and tripe every two weeks without fail. When I get back, I'm going to serve her chitlins. I think she'll like them. It must have killed her to throw away that part of the chicken."

"Brains and tripe! Oh, Lord, girl! And chitlins is from pigs, not chickens."

A few weeks later, a 1945 Buick pulled up in front of the little house on Sycamore, and out stepped "Slick" in his white Navy dress uniform. Esther and Mum were sitting outside on the only step from the sidewalk to the house, smoking Rudy's cigarettes.

"Esther, this is my husband," Mum said. "You know, the bastard who hasn't been around to see if his wife and daughter were alive or dead."

"Nice to meet you," said Esther, tucking her long legs under her so not to trip him. "I'm going inside, Peggy. I'll see you later."

"OK, Esther, thanks for the cigarette." She turned to my father. "Whose car is that?"

"Mine," he answered. "I needed a car."

"You didn't need a car; you could take the bus to work or walk, like I do. And where did you get the money for that car?"

"I put down a deposit and got a car loan. Everyone has a car loan."

"Oh, really? Do they now? And where did you get the deposit? Was it, perhaps, out of a little box with a mother-of-pearl lid with a rose engraved on the top?"

"It's for us, so what the difference? We can take nice rides in the country and go on picnics."

"I don't want to go for rides or bloody picnics, and the difference is that you stole it from me."

"I am the man, and I am the one working."

"Well my dear husband, you are not the only one who works, if I had waited for you, both of us—there are two of us remember—would have starved to death. I don't have a fancy car; I walk everywhere, grateful to have a bloody job so we can eat"

"You sat around at my folks all day, aggravating them with your temper tantrums, making fun of their spiritual religion. I couldn't take it anymore, and then you move into nigger town. My nerves are not over the war yet, but I'm back now, and I am willing to start over again."

"I called you, and they always said you were out in the field. I bet you were in the bloody field alright. What? Did your girlfriend kick you out, or did you steal all her money too?"

My mother told me they were shouting at each other on the street and I had started to cry, she picked me up and walked into the house. My father followed us through the little house, down the narrow hallway, to the last door on the left that opened up to the small room that had been our home for the past few months. Loud music came from Esther's phonograph, a kind, thoughtful gesture to drown out the arguments. Esther knew this would embarrass her friend, but she kept her ear pressed against the wall anyway, just in case she needed to answer a call for help.

The room was scrubbed and smelled of soap. There was a small vase of dandelions and tiny blue wildflowers that she'd picked through the broken concrete on the sidewalk as she walked home from work. Mrs. Merry's borrowed quilts and blankets were folded neatly on the end of the iron bed that doubled as a couch during the day. We slept together, my mother and me, on this narrow bed against the wall, she on one end, and me on the other, her legs protecting me from falling on the floor.

My mother walked right into the corner where she had made a makeshift kitchen, and grabbed a saucepan from the cupboard—an open wood crate that Rudy had nailed to the wall. She flung the pan in Hart's face, and then she sat on the floor and cried her beautiful face twisted with despair. All of this time, neither of them looked at me, sitting in a corner, shaking. My father walked over and picked up my mother, gambling that she would cling to him after months of a sad, longing loneliness. He won.

Our earliest memories are at what age? Is it the same for everyone, or is it a perceived traumatic event, regardless of age, that will always stay with us and lurks around, jumping out uninvited many years later? I can be reading an unrelated novel, or doing the most mundane daily chores, and I can be transformed to the little room in Wichita, Kansas, as if the last fifty-seven years didn't happen. I am that child, shaking, looking at my protector, who is throwing a pot at a man whom I am not sure I have seen before. He is not dressed like Rudy, the only other man I know. He has sticks, coloured stripes pinned to his coat. They look like candy, and I want to touch them. I am scared of this man who is holding my mother.

Esther gently knocked at the door a few hours later. She was wearing a brown fur coat that she said Rudy had brought home from his last business trip.

"Oh, Esther, I would love a coat like that. You really do look better than the bloody Queen of England." My mother glanced over at my father, who was getting the message that if she were to get a coat like this, there was a possibility he would be forgiven. Later, my father and Rudy struck some sort of a deal in the hallway, for Rudy not only got a brown fur coat like Esther's for my mother but also a little white fur for me, with a matching muff. It was much too big for me, a child who was barely walking, but it was put away for me to "grow into".

Everyone seemed happy with the way things worked out, even Esther, in spite of the fact that now she wouldn't be the only one with a brown fur coat. But she was proud of her businessman, Rudy, who could put everything right with our world.

The next Saturday night, Esther and Peggy walked into the Blue Note with matching fur coats—Peggy, with her fresh Toni perm, and Esther, with a black hat. When Billie Holiday came to the Blue Note and played with Dizzy Gillespie, Esther and Peggy insisted on the front table and glared at the other tables that dared even a side glance of disapproval at the two couples, one black and the other white. My mother leaned over and told Esther that if Chips Rafferty had been in the Blue Note and saw them dressed in their fur coats, they would be surely be in his next movie.

The day after my father pulled up in his new Buick, the little money box with the mother-of-pearl lid was dropped off in the safe-keeping of the only person my mother trusted in America. Mrs. Merry now had the added burden of being the trustee of the little box. Every payday, when Mum would pay her the small amount for babysitting, Mrs. Merry would insist she put some of what was left in the box.

For a while, my father came home every night. He liked the pulse of the neighbourhood, the music and the cheerful shouting, the excited screams from the kids playing in the street. He thought perhaps that Rudy would include him on his business deals, but Esther told Mum that Rudy said there was something he didn't like about this man, and that Esther should tell her friend to be careful. Rudy was a good judge of people and the streets, Esther said. He was "a well-travelled man", she said, holding her chin up proudly. So after a month, the predictable boredom propelled my father to other places of his own special interest, and we were alone most nights and week-ends again.

Dear Glad,

Hope you are well, as we are here. Hart is not home too much; he goes and leaves me every night. He comes home from work, eats dinner, gets dressed up like a bloody galah, and goes out. Says he is going to meet his mates, or buddies, as he calls them. Don't know why he needs to take a bath, shave, and get all dressed up for a bunch of old Navy mates. Sometimes he doesn't come home all night, and if I didn't have Esther and Rudy in the front of the house, I would be scared. I try not to bother them, and I am usually tired. Sometimes we go out to the supper clubs with Esther and Rudy, and it reminds me of nights out in Sydney. The coloured people are the only ones who know how to have a good time here; dancing and singing and laughing comes so easy to them, despite all the struggles. Battlers, they are, in the true meaning of the word. So glad that Sister Ann told me to get a trade and got me the job to learn the book-binding business. We had to buy Hart a car; he can't take the bus or walk, like I do. So that took all the money we saved for our move back to Australia. I miss it so much. What I would give right now to be down at the quay, having a hamburger, sitting on the steps at the Ship Inn Pub. The hamburgers are different over here—no egg, no beetroot. Thanks for sending the five pounds; I will pay you back, but luv, don't send any more; it's only worth a few dollars here.

Diana is growing big and talking like a bloody Yank. My father would roll over in his grave if he heard her. She stays with Mrs. Merry every day while I work and sometimes doesn't want to come home when I go to get her. The winter is coming, and they said we should get snow. I have never seen snow, but when I get paid—I am getting a raise—I am going to put a pair of snow boots on lay-by (they call it "lay-away" here). The women that I work with are very nice and stick up for one another. If one of us has a hangover or a bad period, they help her out and work harder. Most Americans are always smiling; I like that about them. I didn't go to Mass last Sunday. Hart couldn't get out of bed to take me. The closest Catholic Church is miles away. Not too many Catholics here; they say there are more in Boston. Not sure where that is, but I might like to go there—no, no, no, I just want to come home. Sometimes I am scared that I will end up liking it here, or giving up. Esther said I could go with her to the Gospel Baptist. I didn't tell her that it's a sin for Catholics to go to another church. I wanted to go with her; she dresses better than Queen Mary and comes home happy, singing and dancing all the way up the yard. You should see her jitterbug. I taught her the old Charleston, and she taught me the jitterbug. Remember when we were kids, and we did the Black Bottom in the yard? We used to love to say "Black bottom". Well, must sign off to get this posted. Love to your family. Would you go around and see how Mumma is doing?

I try to tell Mumma that I am doing good and everything is hunky-dory; bloody lie, that is, but if I told her the truth, how I hate it here and what a bloody bludger Hart can be, she would find some way to blame poor Dadda. I just know she would.

Bye for now.

Your loving friend,

Peggy

Dear Mumma,

How are you? We are doing just "swell", as they say here in America. Hart is working hard, and we have a nice little flat with a vegetable and flower garden. Diana is getting big and says OK to everything, in an American accent. I have a lovely fur coat that Hart bought for me, and Diana has a lovely white fur coat and muff that she will grow into. We are looking forward to seeing snow soon and wearing these coats. I am going to Mass every Sunday, and then after Mass we go and have a big dinner with Hart's family. I miss you, Mumma, and hope we can take a holiday in Australia soon.

Your loving daughter,

Peggy

In Mrs. Merry's backyard

We lived for another year at the back of Esther's house. (It really wasn't her house, but it made no difference; we never saw the landlord.) Esther took a small amount for the room, and as long as we weren't evicted, who cared?

Returning servicemen were able to get a house with little or no down payment after the war. Towns across America were in a building frenzy. We moved into our own house outside of the city, far away from Esther's laughter, and Mrs. Merry's corn cob wine, and

Rudy's endless enterprises. I don't know too much about the next two years; my mother never told me. It seems those years didn't deserve to take up space in my mother's memory.

Before we left the "Negro section" of Wichita, Mrs. Merry refused to give my mother the mother-of-pearl box and its contents unless she promised to put it in the bank. Her promise was not enough; words were cheap, she said, so we all went to the bank that day: Benny, Thomas, Willie, Teddy, and me, with Mrs. Merry and my mother.

"I told you on that first day when you was sittin on the sidewalk, a woman should always have her own money that no one should know about."

"How did you ever become so smart?" my mother said trying to find a seat in the bank for all of us.

"The Lord made me smart. He said to me one day, Mary Alice, learn from life. Be kind, and I will always help you."

"He didn't say that! When did He appear to you? I didn't think He appeared to Baptists."

"He is in the heart of everyone. Sometimes they don't want to look down into their hearts, even murderers."

"I don't want to talk about murderers. Tell me, how come you have a house and don't seem as poor as the other Negroes on Sycamore Street?"

"I am blessed more than most other folks. That's why they leave the children at my door, and that's why I take them in. See that young white man sitting at the desk, who said good morning to me and tipped his hat? He's a gentleman and the president of this bank."

"So what?" my mother said straining to get a look at this well dressed man who was glancing every few seconds in our way with an uncomfortable smile.

"Well, I used to work for his daddy and had a child when I was fifteen. Her name was Sadie; that was my mother's name, Sadie. Sadie, Sadie, my darling little Sadie."

"Where is she?"

"The Lord come and took her. You know that Lord that don't show Himself to Baptists; she died with the fever."

"I'm sorry. I bet she's with Our Blessed Lady. She'll take care of her till you get there, but how did you get that house? Esther rents from a white landlord; you don't have a landlord?"

"His daddy owns the house," she said, pointing to the bank

president, "and I can live in it until I die."

"Was that blackmail?"

"No, baby, more like *white* male, and always remember the old proverb: the Lord helps those who help themselves."

In the late forties, Americans were trying to put the war behind them. Women, who competently filled the labour demands of war industries as well as positions vacated by millions of men and women who had entered military service, were expected to give up these independent roles and return to submissive domesticity, regardless of whether or not they liked it. Most of them cheerfully donned aprons and got down to the business of making up for lost time, filling their homes with apple pies and kids. After World War II, America was in a better economic condition than any other country in the world and vowed to take care of its returning veterans. The GI Bill of Rights that was passed in 1944 provided money for veterans to buy homes and farms and to attend college, thus bettering themselves—and having children in unprecedented numbers. Of course, not all Americans were able to participate in these opportunities, and the economic prosperity was largely lost on the minorities, namely African Americans, Hispanics, Native Americans, and women. Their exclusion would lead to a more aggressive struggle to win the full freedoms and civil rights, as guaranteed to them by the Declaration of Independence and the US Constitution, a struggle that continues.

Saying goodbye to Esther and Mrs. Merry hinted at finality that my mother refused to accept, and she promised to stop by once a week. Clutching her Frank Sinatra record, fur coat, and the recipe for corn cob wine, she said good-bye to the only two people who had made her hopeful and happy. We drove away with one car load, off to the suburbs and the American dream—a house with a thirty-year mortgage, a car, and a neighbourhood without coloureds. We even had a pressure cooker.

The three of us, 1947

It would be the unhappiest time of Peggy's life. Gone were the Hollywood Saturdays, laughing with her friend, and the corn cob wine that would be waiting for her every day after work. I screamed every day as I was dropped off at nursery school close to our house, and for a month I refused to take off my coat, staying in a corner and began sucking my thumb. Mum tried to continue working, but the plan of driving in to the city with my father lasted only a few months and ended when he didn't show up one night and left her sitting on the steps of the printing factory for three hours. Rudy driving by saw her on the step; he offered to get me from nursery school while she waited for my father. When a coloured man came to pick me up, two hours after the school closed, the owner said I was never to return. She was running a respectable place for children and was going to keep it that way. Children had to be picked up before 5:30 and not by coloureds. My arms tightened around Rudy's neck, wrinkling his expensive silk suit. He patted me on the back, and we walked away.

Peggy blamed herself, she said. She thought that maybe it was her fault that they couldn't be happy like other married couples, like the one's she saw in the vacuum cleaner ads: the man, sitting on the couch, smiling, reading the paper, while his wife pushed a vacuum around, wearing her pearls, with her hair tied up in a scarf, as she looked fondly at the two children, a boy and a girl, playing on the carpet. Peggy always complained about going home, but maybe if she would try to be like a real wife, Hart would come home every night. The next day, she left the printing factory, saying good-bye to the bindery women and the supervisor that had hired her.

"You're a good worker," the supervisor told her, "and if you ever want to come back, you always have a job here. But a woman does belong at home, raising a family."

Dear Glad,

If this house was in Sydney, I would be very happy to live in it the rest of my life. It's a nice little house, but I think it was put up in a hurry. I joined the Australian Wives Club, and we take turns meeting at each other's houses. We drink billy tea and eat Arnott's biscuits. Someone always has something Australian sent over by their family, and they share it. It's good to talk about home, and our life growing up, and who is going to take a trip back soon.

My friend Doreen from Brisbane told me that her husband told her that Hart has been in the government office cafeteria with a woman every day, and he kisses her when he leaves. She said if it was her, she would want to know. When he came home, I threw my good cut-glass sugar bowl at him. He laughed and said they were only friends. I am trying so hard to be a cheerful wife and a good cook. I burn everything and blew up the pressure cooker. How can anyone blow up a bloody pressure cooker? The lid came flying off, and the peas and potatoes were all on the ceiling. Well, nothing new here; life isn't much fun, but chin up, and love to your mum and dad.

Had a letter from Mumma; she says she has been a bit crook with a cold. Would you go over and cheer her up?

Your loving friend,

Peggy.

When my father was home, he started to take a sudden interest in his daughter, and on Saturdays, with the pretence of giving my mother a rest, he would take me fishing or to the park. To say that I remember the reported fondling would be a lie; I don't, and when I visit the darkest parts of my earliest childhood memories, I cannot dig deep enough to honestly pull out from my mind's remote corner anything other than his cruel indifference. I remember him locking me in a dark closet, his strange way of disciplining a three-year-old, but to only guess at a possible repressed memory of his sexual caress would be stretching into a possible murky lie. In my later years as a teenager I only talked to my father a few times and it was horrible. He seemed to have a need to always bring the conversation back to when I was a child and what he would do to me. He talked in a hushed voice and seemed to get sick pleasure in reliving those times; he was evil, and I would hang up on him shaking, unable to understand why my father would want to hurt me so. I was never able to tell me my mother of these incidents as she stood by beaming at the fact that her efforts to remain in contact with this man who she had neatly labelled through the years as a victim of circumstances of the war. Her interpretations of my sobbing, she believed, to be sadness at not being a family. My confusion as to her fantasy was mixed with a feeling of misplaced guilt-that somehow it was my duty to keep our lives as normal as possible. I knew in those later years I would have to deal with her denial. If I told her the things he said to me, I thought that somehow I would be blamed. She had adopted a "kill the messenger mentality" through the years as a way of dealing with unpleasant news. I subconsciously sometime in my immature years slipped into a steadfast role of the shield, protecting her from more of life's burdens.

Fortunately back in those early days in Kansas she must have started to suspect his unnatural affection for children—and at that time in her life she was wise enough to know there was no time for doubt.

It was better to be wrong and safe than to have her baby hurt. She would have to believe the worst. Her inner struggle between loving my father and her protective maternal instincts was probably the hardest thing she ever faced. Her life would have its hardships, but the struggles that she was to face would be so easy compared to the realization that my father, the man she had planned a life around, was a paedophile. She thought about the warnings from Grandma Lucy, Rudy's expressed concerns to Esther, Mrs. Merry's insisting that she have her own money, and even his own father, Milton's, warnings. She had a little money in the bank, but in the meantime, she never let me out of her sight when my father was around while calculating her return to live again in Esther's house.

Hail Mary, full of grace ...

The cable came two weeks later:

YOUR MOTHER PASSED AWAY THIS MORNING AT
MATER HOSPITAL.
WILL TAKE CARE OF ARRANGEMENTS. LETTER
FOLLOWING. MY
DEEPEST SYMPATHY.

LOVE GLADYS

My father went out again that night, leaving us alone, my mother grieving, with a child who couldn't comfort her. She felt that so many things had been left unsaid to a woman with a heart so big as to adopt a baby from a mad woman in 1921.

Dear Peggy,

I have stored some of your mother's furniture. You can decide what you want to do with it. I have all the pictures and letters that she kept and, of course, your adoption papers. I also found quite a bit of money hidden in a teapot. It's enough to pay your passage home, if you so wish. It will be in safe keeping at my mum's until you decide if you want me to send it. I think she was planning a visit to you, as she had just bought a new suitcase. The funeral was small, but you would have been pleased with the Requiem Mass. Fr. O'Brien said some kind words about her being a strong woman.

If you come home I will show you exactly where she is buried; it's a short tram ride from here, and we will go put flowers on the grave.

Hope everything is going good for you both. Have you met any film stars yet?

Your loving friend,

Gladys

My dearest friend Gladys,

Thank you for everything. What would I have ever done without you? It's time for me to come home. Please don't send the money here. Go down to Matson Lines Shipping and book passage for us, San Francisco to Sydney, on the next ship. I have enough to take a train to San Francisco, with maybe a little left until I get a job. So much to tell you, but I am so tired, and it will wait.

Love,

Peggy

A month later we said good-bye to Mrs. Merry, Benny, Willie, Teddy, and Thomas. I clung to Mrs. Merry's neck and buried my face in that big, warm, safe bosom. We never said good-bye to Esther or Rudy; they had left the house, according to Mrs. Merry, "in a hurry one night, just before four policemans got there. Just waved good-bye to me as they was running down the street".

"She always talked about going to Harlem and the Cotton Club," Peggy said. "Maybe that's where they are, and anyway, I hope she gets there."

"She'll get nowhere but jail with that Rudy. They said he's been robbin' fur coats from the big department stores."

"Rudy was a kind man, always treated me good. Maybe he did what he had to do."

"What he has to do in this life," Mrs. Merry said, "is just be a righteous man." She looked somewhat satisfied that her prediction of his demise had come about.

Mum told me that she walked over to the little house on Sycamore Street for one last look at the step where Esther would sit with her chocolate brown legs spread in front of her, a flower always tucked behind her ear, a haughty, defiant look on her beautiful face, with its high cheekbones and big brown eyes. She thought of the times in the backyard when they had their Hollywood Days, Esther's hair in rags, Mum's in skinny grey curlers, drinking the corn cob whiskey and giggling. And the time they both ran over and peed on the next-door neighbour's garden after she told them they laughed too loud and were two "no good hussies". And Mum had told Esther, "Look, Esther, our pee is the same colour."

Two women from such different worlds, who became close friends in a few months and had laughed and peed together.

MRS. MERRY'S CORN COB WINE

12 raw corn on the cob
1 gallon boiling water
2 packages yeast
9 cups sugar

Pour boiling water over corn cobs in a large container and cover with a cloth, and let stand for 24 hours. Take the corn cobs out and add the yeast and sugar. Cover loosely again, and let stand for 9—12 days. Strain through cheesecloth, cover again with a cloth over the container, and store in cool place for 10 weeks. Then it should be ready to drink.

6

THE FUNCTIONAL FAMILY

My father accepted our departure with indifference—or perhaps relief. He told his family that we were just going for a visit to Australia. Sometimes I think my mother wanted to believe that he would join us in Sydney after he "got help". She would say through the years that the war does strange things to people. That may be true, but I don't believe that paedophilia has been proven to be one of those strange things.

We took trains from Wichita to San Francisco, the same route that a few years before had carried this beautiful, young, hopeful woman, dressed in a linen suit, excited to meet her new in-laws and her life in the land of movie stars, Toni perms, and pressure cookers.

50 Brides Return; U.S. Not Like the Movies

> BRISBANE, Monday—More than 50 Australian brides of American servicemen returned by the *Matsonia* today, some homesick and others apparently disappointed because they found the United States not always "like the movies or the magazine advertisements."
>
> Among the women were divorcees, widows, and some who were "just fed up with America."
>
> Some of the women said they felt American women resented their arrival as brides of U.S. servicemen. Others found everything in American moving at an exhausting pace. Other simply said they had made a mistake and wanted to forget about it.
>
> *(Sydney Morning Herald, 23 October 1945)*

I was almost four by the time we were on our way back to Australia, and I'd only had known the kindness of Mrs. Merry and her boys, who were my only playmates. On that train journey to

San Francisco, there was a black family, and I ran over to play with a little boy who seemed about Benny's age. We shared candy and a toy as my mother looked on. A tall white man approached her, his finger almost touching her face as he pointed at her. "I can tell you're a foreigner," he said. "We don't do that in this country, let white children play with niggers."

"Go sit down, you bloody poofter," she said, and she spat on his suit. Because of the kindness she received from Esther and Mrs. Merry and their love of life, which was never jaded by their hardships, Peggy always would be critical of America for the abominable treatment of its black race. Through the years, black athletes would be sent to Australia to represent the U.S. in various sports events.

"Sure," she would say, "they send them out to be winners for America, but in their own country they can't even drink out of the same bloody bubbler" (water fountain).

Oddly, she also refused to listen to anyone who was critical of Australia, which, at the time, supported an official racist policy.

From the 1890s, Australia's government barred non-white people from its continent. Originally, the policy was born out of white miners' resentment towards the industrious Chinese, who were undercutting white labour prices in the 1850s; Chinese were excluded from all Australian colonies by 1888.

"The doctrine of the equality of man was never intended to apply to equality of the Englishman and the Chinaman," declared the then prime minister, Edmund Harton. The policy continued, fuelled by the opposition of labourers in the sugar cane fields of Queensland. The sugar cane workers from Melanesia had been forcibly removed from their homes. This practice was known as blackbirding, and the leaders of Australia vowed to stop this human trafficking. Around seven thousand Islanders were deported in the 1890s. Only white labourers were then allowed to work in the fields. While the trade unions and their affiliate political party was the driving force for white Australia, the main focus was to keep Australia racially pure. In the Commonwealth Parliamentary Debates, on September 12, 1901, Chris Watson, the leader of the Labour Party, stated: "The objection I have to the mixing of these coloured people with the white people of Australia—although I admit it is, to a large extent, tinged with a consideration of an industrial nature—lies … in the possibility and probability of racial contamination."

It was not until 1975 that the Racial Discrimination Act banned and deemed illegal the use of racial criteria for any official purpose.

While America was struggling with Civil Rights in the 1960s, the Australian Aborigine was not given the right to vote or other rights of citizenship until 1967. Like the Native Americans, the full-blooded Aborigines had been expected to die out from disease and deplorable living conditions in their remote desert settlements. The similarities of the treatment and white European society's attitude toward indigenous people were the same in America and Australia. Their hoped demise and extinction would be assisted by introducing them to alcohol, poisoned water and lacing their flour with strychnine.

A group of about one hundred thousand Aboriginal children, from 1910 until the early 1970s, were forcibly removed from their families in what is now referred to as the "Stolen Generation". While the children were generally of mixed race, with mostly white fathers or grandfathers, the goal was to make them part of white society. One of these children was Henry Penrith, who was born in 1936 and would later become a fighter for Aborigine rights. Penrith was taken from his Aboriginal father and sent to an orphanage, where he suffered floggings with a cattle whip. On one of many disciplinary occasions, his punishment for breaking a window with a cricket ball was to stand in front of the class and repeat, "Look at me, and you will see that I am an Aborigine". He became an excellent student, attended law school, served in the Agriculture Department of the State of New South Wales and, in the mid-1960s, chose a life of political action. One of his most defiant gestures was during 1988, Australia's bicentennial year. With dignitaries in London and Canberra praising the great Australian nation, he climbed the Cliffs of Dover and planted the red, yellow, and black Australian Aboriginal flag. He made a barbed speech, alluding to the treatment of the Aborigines by the English. He promised that no harm would come to the English native people from his invasion; he wouldn't poison their water, lace their flour with strychnine, or introduce them to alcohol and toxic drugs. It is believed he set the stage for the referendum that amended the Constitution, which finally gave the Aborigine the right to vote. He adopted the name Burnum Burnum meaning "great warrior", from his great-grandfather, a warrior of the Wurundjeri tribe.

Every Christmas, for many years, we sent Mrs. Merry a box of white Irish linen handkerchiefs. We would get a Christmas card in June, delayed because of insufficient postage to send air mail. If one postage stamp could get a letter to anywhere in America, then she believed two stamps could get a letter anywhere out of America, and it eventually did. There was never any news about Esther in the letters, but Mum had no doubt she was now the Queen of Harlem.

"I bet Esther is knocking them dead when she walks in to that Cotton Club," she would say, needing to believe Esther was happy and where she had always wanted to be; hearing the words made it so.

Mrs. Merry lived a long time, raised a lot of "righteous men"—and some not so righteous. It was many years later that my mother received a letter from one of the righteous ones:

Dear Peggy,

Mama died last month and went home to Jesus. Her big old heart was tired. I found all your letters, and she had them all wrapped in a ribbon. I am working as a janitor for a big aircraft company here in Wichita and keep the factory floor real clean; they said some day I will be in charge of all the cleaning men. Teddy is in jail. I go see him when I can. He cried when I told him Mama died. Willie and Thomas moved somewhere north, don't know where. I still remember you and Princess, so long ago. I have a daughter; her name is Mary Alice. We called her after Mama, and she got to see her before she died.

Love,

Benny

Grandma Eunice sent me a birthday card and five dollars every year until I was thirty-two. Lionel never did come home from the war. Grandpa Milton died long before Eunice; they found him with in his wood shop with a whiskey bottle in one hand and a centrefold from *Playboy* magazine in the other.

After a month crossing the Pacific, we sailed into the Heads of Sydney Harbour, the cliffs enfolding us like warm, soft angel wings. Gladys was waving from the dock, a beacon once again with her bright red hair. We looked like we stepped out of Hollywood, glamorous but sweating in our fur coats under the already scorching Australian sun. We waited for one of the roaming society photographers from the *Daily Telegraph*—it was a practice for them to greet arriving ships and try to fill a page of pictures with arrivals and departures. Not able to resist my mother's smile and a toddler in a white fur coat, we were propped up on a cargo crate, while Gladys looked on proudly at her friend and told everyone passing by who would listen, "That's my friend; she's been in America, and her picture is going to be in the society pages". They would use the same caption for all arrivals, just changing the names: "Peggy Dailey and daughter, Diana, arrive in Sydney for a visit with Mrs. Dailey's parents."

But there were no parents left, no family home, and only enough money to live for a few months, at the most. These matters were of no importance on that day. We were back in Sydney, where the temperature rarely gets below fifty degrees, wearing stolen fur coats and with a suitcase full of Toni permanent waves. Looking up from the water's edge to the old rock's neighbourhood, my mother said she pictured her father looking down from the small hill, with his mailbag and wearing his familiar grey blue uniform, smiling and waving. "Good on ya, luv. You made it home."

The euphoria of being back in her beloved city with her best friend and an ocean between her and the man she had married gave Peggy the freedom to fabricate a love that she would eventually come to believe had existed. Perhaps the hints she witnessed of his unnatural penchant for children was a figment of her imagination when her mind was visited by the devil. His glazed fixation on children thrown in his company by friends and family was perhaps nothing more than natural affection, as he patted them slowly from their face down to their knees, a pure fondness for their innocence. He would from then on take a place in her life and her mind as the "poor bugga whose mind was never the same after that bloody war". When Eunice called some years later to say that my father, this man who was now exalted to a war victim, had been arrested and put in jail for "solicitation of a minor for an immoral act", she yelled at her and told her "it was all a pack of lies".

Post-war Australia was experiencing a housing shortage that became a harsh reality to my mother, who had over-stayed her welcome after a few weeks with each friend. She would stick her nose in and comment on their family business, which was none of her own.

"I would do it this way."

"Don't take that from him."

"Don't let that bludger talk to you like that."

We needed to find our own home and allow generous friends to have privacy in the early fragile years of marriage.

As America went so did Australia in an effort to reinvent itself after World War II, believing that population growth was essential for a good economic future and experiencing a large-scale migration boom. Millions of people in Europe were displaced from their homelands and many of the war weary were encouraged to move to Australia by the lure of government-assisted passage. Combined with the return of the soldiers resuming their pre-war roles, the influx of migration, and the marriage boom, it was almost impossible for a single woman with a child to find affordable housing.

My mother's new place in society was as a "deserted wife". The social stigma attached to divorced, single women and unwed mothers were further encouraged by the attitude of the country. The social ideal was the employed father and the domestic-driven mother, caring for her husband and two or more children in a modern suburban home. Enhanced by the media images at the time, women were made to believe they had failed to live up to standards of responsible behaviour if they were not engaged in the sacred profession of homemaker. Their self-image was scarred, as they wore the belief that it was their fault that somehow they weren't as good as the women who were in those homes, supported by a man and society's approval. This illusory ideal social scenario was buoyed by the high level of male employment, with a wage system based on a family wage for men, rather than equal pay for women.

As my mother said many times to her complaining friends in the same position, "It's no use whingeing about it; it's a man's world, even if he's a lazy bugga. And it's not going to change, until we grow a dick, so go on with your life." Usually, these conversations ended up with their laughing hysterically between puffs on a cigarette and sips of beer.

"How do you grow a dick?" one of them would say.

"I think you have to fart a lot."

"And tell lots of lies."

"And burp."

Sydney's housing shortage created high rents, and without the support of a family, the dilemma of what to do with a child while she worked two jobs to pay such rent was probably one of the hardest obstacles Peggy would ever face. There were no day-care centres or nursery schools, only Children's Homes. The Homes were already bursting at the seams with orphans and war-torn migrant children sent from Europe by a well-meaning international social system. Other children absorbed into the Homes were left there by desperate and abandoned mothers who couldn't find the means to care for them.

Despite the many individual reasons that these children had come to live in the Homes, all were quickly and neatly labelled "neglected children". That condescension would always determine their place in a society that respected the social standing of a family, and those children would bear that class distinction. Entitled by their efforts in making provisions for the physical care of those neglected "gutter" children, the guardians of the Children's Homes indulged and rewarded themselves with the euphoria of superiority, and that would transcend into the minds of the "neglected" and forever remain there.

"You can leave her here; we do have an opening for a four-year-old, but in order for the child to adjust, there can be no visits for three months," said the director of a Children's Home in Sydney.

"I can't do that; she's my baby," Peggy responded. "She would be so frightened if she didn't see me for all that time and maybe she would forget all about me. Can't I come and pick her up on Friday nights and bring her back Sunday night?"

"Well, I'm sorry, it's the best for the child, and if you're not willing to do that, I am very busy and have other people to see. We have a long waiting list of mothers who care enough for their children to understand what's best for them when they are unable to take care of them."

"Thank you very much," Peggy said, "but I won't be leaving her here."

My mother would later say that I tugged on her skirt, saying, "Mummy, please don't leave me in this big house."

"Never, darling, never, never, never."

"I want to go to stay with Mrs. Merry."

"Mrs. Merry is in America, a long way away." *Oh, God, I wish I had her here with me*, she thought. *She would just sit me down, pour a glass of corn liquor, and make me laugh as she stomped around the kitchen with her big bum and bigger bosom, and then just tell me what to do.*

Passing through the big gates of the Children's Home, Peggy walked quickly, dragging me along, as if to get away from that place as fast as she could. In a familiar park, close to the race track, she sat on a bench. "Hail Mary, full of grace ..."

The answer to her prayers came on cue, but this time it wasn't a big, black angel in a red dress. It was Teddy Lane, an old neighbourhood friend from Peggy's teenage years in Zetland, who stood in front of her, holding four leashes of greyhound dogs.

"Is that you Peggy? I don't bloody believe it! Where the bloody hell have you been? I haven't seen you for years. You're still a good sort, beautiful as ever. Heard you married a bloody Yank. Is this your little girl?"

Peggy looked up, amazed. "Teddy, it has been years! Are you still living in Waterloo? Yes, this is my daughter. We just got back from America. I'm looking for someone to mind her while I work, till my husband comes to join us. He is going to when he gets some business settled." Peggy could hardly believe her friend was standing there. "God, Teddy, remember the times we had when we were kids, and you lived on the other side of the lane? We used to pinch lollies from the old Greek's grocery store." It seemed so long ago but it really wasn't, and Peggy started to cry.

"Aw, luv, don't cry," Teddy said soothingly. "Let me talk to my sister, Dot; maybe she could help you out. You remember Dot; she's a little older than us and was always haughty, but she's a good woman. She never married, and she took care of our mother. We all live together up in Newcastle now. I am down here racing greyhounds at the track over there. Give me your address, and I'll talk to Dot. You could take the train up every week-end till your daughter gets older and you get on your feet, you know? Or ..." he added, as a kind afterthought, "When your husband joins you."

My mother told me many times that she felt it was futile to give Teddy her address, but she did anyway. She hardly knew Dot, who had been much older and seemed so posh and wasn't around the neighbourhood too much. Why would someone who was taking care of her mother want to take on a kid from someone she hardly knew? She would have to be a saint or a crazy woman; in either case, Peggy didn't think it would be a decision she'd have to face.

A week later a letter arrived:

Dear Peggy,

Talked to Dot, and she said let's give it a try. Bring your daughter up next Friday night with her clothes. It's good country air up here, and we have plenty of room. Get off the train in Cardiff, the one that stops at every station, arriving at 7:30. We will be there to meet you.

Regards,

Ted

Many times in later years they would tell me the story of that Sunday night, when it was time for my mother to leave and go back to Sydney, and I cried.

"Now, darling, be brave. You're going to be safe here with Auntie Dot."

"It's hard to be brave," I said.

"You're Australian, and Australians are brave and don't cry."

I shook my head. "I'm not Australian; I'm a bloody Yank."

I lived with this wonderful family for the next eight years. I was to call them Uncle Ted and Auntie Dot. An idyllic past isn't worth writing about and sometimes can hardly be remembered. There were no beatings or abuse that I could use as an excuse for my bad behaviour later in life. I guess there wasn't much money, but who knew? Certainly not me. For the rest of my life I would lovingly refer to them as Auntie Dot and Uncle Ted. Auntie Dot made me dolls out of rags, just like Mrs. Merry had done. Uncle Ted came home from work in the coal mines with biscuits, and on his pay day he would buy me pink candy pigs made from dyed sugar. I wanted to work in a coal mine when I grew up so that I could get biscuits filled with butter cream and have sugar pigs every pay day. My mother came on the late train every Friday night, stayed the week-end, and paid them two pounds each week for my board. She worked at the *Sun* office during the day and at a series of restaurants at night. She could never pay them enough for the protection and love and warmth they showed me.

Every Saturday night we would have a concert with lots of their relatives. There were only two forms of entertainment: listening to the radio and family concerts. There were no instruments, but Uncle Ted would hold two big spoons and loosely let them flop up and down between the top of his knee and the palm of his left hand. While he played the spoons, his tongue would hang out. He tried to play once with his mouth closed, but it didn't sound the same. After he stopped playing and his tongue went back in his mouth, Auntie Dot would sing "Roses of Picardy" with a faraway look in her eyes. Perhaps she dreamed that she was on stage and singing to an adoring audience who were throwing her roses on the stage. She would have beautiful clothes and many admirers. I would act out my favourite radio serial episode of "Mary Wallace", a poor unfortunate woman who had been banished to the penal colony of Tasmania for some slight infraction. My repertoire always began just as the radio serial, with the judge's harsh words from an English courtroom. The concerts were the same every Saturday night. There was no need to learn new talents or try new songs, as the applause and laughs were always fresh as if hearing "Roses of Picardy" for the first time.

"Roses are growing in Picardy in the hush of the ..."

"Mary Wallace, I now sentence you to ten years in Van Diemen's Land!"

"No! No! No!" would be my reply, while flailing all over the kitchen.

Saturday night concert parties at Auntie Dot's
Me, in the back row

Auntie Dot had been a barmaid at the local pub before she left to take care of various charges and her ailing mother. She said that one day she would return to her career in the "hotel business". In the meantime, she would need to know the current price of beer. On days that we would walk by the pub, she would say to me, "Stay here. Don't move, and don't talk to strangers. I will be back straight away." She was true to her word and would come out within a minute, reciting the latest prices of beer. A shanty (beer and lemonade) was sixpence (pennies), a pony (small glass of beer) was twelve pence, and a schooner (a large glass of beer) was sixteen pence.

"I have to keep my mind ready for when I go to back," she would tell me. We would then play a game of "barmaid and the customer." My role, of course, was the customer who was buying beer from her, and she would add it up in her head, the quicker the better.

"OK, Missus," I would say, pretending we were in a pub to add reality to our game, "I will have two shanties, one schooner, and four ponies for me and me mates over there."

The California bungalow style houses were copied successfully and were conducive to the Australian climate. A front veranda offered shade and protected the bedroom windows, which usually were situated in the front of the house, from the beating sun. We would play "barmaid and the customer" quite often on the veranda of that little house. I tired of this game after a few years and dreaded it when the pub had an increase in beer prices.

Most of all in those days, I felt loved and the centre of everything. Soon, I would not cry when my mother left to go back to Sydney on Sunday nights. She would leave around five o'clock, and I would walk with her halfway to the train station down the hill, as far as the bridge, which was as far as I was allowed. I would wait by the train tracks and wave as her train went by, jumping up and down when I saw her hanging out of the sooty window, yelling, and "See you next week, darling girl!" paying no mind to the train dirt on her white blouse. It was back to her job to earn "a woman's wage", enough to pay the two pounds to Auntie Dot and the rent on her tiny flat. Extra money came when she would work through her holidays, and we would both get a new dress and shoes.

Just as it's then alter ego, the United States, Australia was going through a paranoid fear of Communism, the Cold War, and a widely held perception that any demands from the unions was an effort to promote class conflict and therefore would popularize Communistic leadership. Russia, which had been an ally, with everyone waving Russian flags in the streets of Sydney when Russia entered the war, was now feared, as their strength increasingly dominated Europe.

It was around this time that Auntie Dot decided to marry a Russian, Padrik Poetschka. She had met Pat, as we called him, at a dance at the Returned Soldiers Club. We are not sure if he was born in Russia; he certainly had no accent, and whenever anyone complained of the slightest hardship, he could top it with stories of his hard life on a farm in Tamworth. He changed his name to Pat Pascoe, feeling a need to shed any clue of his Russian ancestry. If it was a romantic, passionate love, they kept it well hidden. So after a courtship that consisted of a few afternoons on the veranda, a town-hall wedding followed on a hot Friday afternoon in February. The bride wore a cream coloured suit, and the groom a grey suit and wide blue tie. A small party followed in the yard, with a keg of beer, a plate of sausage rolls, and lamingtons piled up to resemble a wedding cake. The groom became my Uncle

Pat that day. The next day he cleared out his rented room in Swansea and moved into the little house on Lovell Street, carrying his beat-up brown leather suitcase, a bottle of port wine, and a bunch of roses for his new bride.

Immediately, he surveyed the condition of the neglected garden, and that's when he staked his claim. Silently, he decided which duties he could perform to aesthetically contribute to the household. The garden would always be his territory, digging for days under the hot sun, preparing the neglected dirt for wonderful things to come. When he wasn't working at the steel factory, he was polishing the old black coal stove or digging in the garden. Neither Uncle Ted nor Auntie Dot had an opinion one way or the other; he could do what he wanted, as they never thought much of the garden or cared if the old stove gleamed.

Every Saturday there would be a big pot of soup on the stove, sometimes split pea or barley and usually full of vegetables from his garden. When he boiled vegetables, he made me drink the cooled water, telling me that's where all the vitamins were. A tablespoon of molasses and cod liver oil became part of the daily routine under his care. It wasn't necessary to like it, as it was good for us. No one, even the most casual of visitors, could dodge that big black blob of molasses balanced on a tablespoon, aimed at their face. When I think back now, I know this was his way of loving us. Kisses and saying "I love you" were foreign to us then, and embarrassing. The look of satisfaction on his face after we had a bowl of barley soup, cod liver oil, and molasses was a true silent love. He knew about the dangers of smoking even then, many years before all the public warnings. "Go ahead; kill yourself with those bloody cancer sticks," he would yell at my mother every week-end. "And don't go smoking in the same room as this kid; it's like she's smoking, too."

"You're bloody mad," Peggy would say and go out on the veranda to finish her cigarette.

Uncle Pat was to die years before any of his scolded smokers left this earth. He died of complications from skin cancer. Many days spent in his garden under the hot Australian sun proved to be a bigger enemy than the cancer sticks.

Life was good with the coal miner, his stern but loving sister, and the Russian. My mind always wanders back to them when I hear in today's conversation the ignorant term "dysfunctional family". Would we have been viewed as dysfunctional? Unconventional families were more common after the war, despite Australia's effort to glorify the nuclear family. In most houses, reality wasn't able to accommodate the vision of the post-war, ideal, picture-perfect family that Australia wanted as its model. Displaced families and foster children were an undeniable part of post-war life. Widows couldn't earn a living wage, and deserted women and children of servicemen and unwed mothers made up a large social scrap of the rich tapestry.

Uncle Pat went to work every day on the bus to the steel plant. In another place or time, his creativity and brilliant mind may have been capable of great things. But this was late-1940s Australia; you played the hand you were dealt without "whingeing". His true self flourished in the garden and he was absorbed in world events—reading all the newspapers that came his way. The highlight of his shopping trip into the city would be to visit the Tatler Newsreel Theatre with it's continuous loop of world events, while Auntie Dot went on to David Jones, pretending she could afford all the finery that she so carefully examined. "Let's duck into the Tatler" he would say. I remember sitting in the small theatre, watching a newsreel of a mushroom cloud exploding from a hydrogen bomb—the latest bragging developments from America, making us feel safe that we had such a powerful friend. The garden around the little house began to flourish under Uncle Pat's care. The giant roses, calla lilies, and snap dragons drew attention away from the house that always needed painting. He would mix white and green powder that smelled like rotten fish for the garden, and we would wait for the glorious blooms. I felt the loving protection of my unconventional caretakers, so nothing triggers many memories from those times. Thank God my mother insisted on my attending a Catholic school, or those eight years would be just a blur of happiness.

Dot and Pat, years later
The barmaid and the Russian

7

THE NUN FROM HELL

I started school at age five at the Sisters of Saint Joseph. Sister Mary Helena was my kindergarten and first-grade teacher. Her red face would get redder underneath a tight, starched head dress, and while walking up and down the aisles she would gravitate towards the side window, her big, black rosary beads jangling, warning us of her approach. She wore black stockings and three layers of heavy clothing in a climate that sometimes reached 110 degrees Fahrenheit. Despite her discomfort, Sister Helena was always smiling, and patted our heads as she floated by our small wooden desks, stopping on her way to the window, hoping for a breeze from the southerly wind to whip around her face. With my newly acquired skill of counting, I could count the one, two, three layers of clothing visible when sitting at her feet. She taught us the alphabet, the sign of the cross, how to count and subtract by taking and adding from large wooden beads that were threaded through wire. Prayers were taught and repeated throughout the day, instilling over and over again into our young minds the Hail Mary, Our Father, and the Act of Contrition. When my classmate Sandra was called upon to say the sign of the cross, she stood up proudly, smiled and said, "Humpty Dumpty sat on the wall." Sandra wasn't listening when we said our prayers and preferred the "other fairy tales".

"No, pet," Sister said. "Humpty Dumpty is not a prayer." Sister Helena turned to hide her face, while shaking with hysterical laughter. Sister Helena's gentle forgiveness of our early bumbling lulled us into a false sense of security of what was to come in the higher grades. Kindergarten and first class were taught together downstairs, while second through sixth were upstairs. The upstairs kids called us "little bubbas" and teased us about being little dunces. When the time came to leave Sister Helena's class and go upstairs, my friend Sandra and I plotted how we would run away from school, live in the gins' camp with the Aborigines, and no one would ever find us. The children's books of "Snugglepot and Cuddlepie," a series about two live nuts from a gum tree, showed us an ideal outback life: no vegetables, no Sisters of St. Joseph, and days full of playing among the wattle and waratahs.

We feared going upstairs. We had seen the second class and feared Sister Chanel more than the Communists. Sometimes Sister Helena would send Sandra and me on an errand upstairs to get more chalk or to deliver a note. If we had to go on an errand to the second class, we held on tightly to each other's hand. Sister Mary Chanel was the second class teacher, and she would glare at us like the evil stepmother in my Little Golden Book of *Hansel and Gretel*. In the corner of the classroom, propped up against the wall, was a piece of round cane, the diameter of a quarter and about five feet long.

Playground rumours were that she would beat kids with this cane and lock them up, and their mothers and fathers would think that the "gypsies" had stole them on their way home from school. They were never seen again but were sent to France (because it sounded so far from Australia) to live their life as slaves, cleaning convents. According to her pupils who would occasionally let us into their circle of whispers, if she was really angry and you did something wrong, she would give you what was referred to as a "sixa"—that meant six whacks with the cane on your out stretched palm. There was, however, a way to avoid that sting from her cane. If you picked a piece of wild fern, opened up the stem, and rubbed your hand with the milky liquid, then your hand would be immune to the pain—a tribute to the not-yet-stifled imagination of children. I never had a chance to try it, as my canings were usually without enough warning or time to start a botanic search. Get caught chewing gum, and it would sit on your nose while you stood in front of the class for an hour. If the boys in her class misbehaved or cried, then they had the additional punishment of either wearing a ribbon in their hair or standing in front of the other children who were allowed to call them "sissies". If children learn by example then some pretty cruel kids probably came from those years of her misguided discipline; certainly, they would have gender confusion.

On the last day of school before our Christmas holidays, Sandra told me that Santa Claus was bringing her a bride doll and a tea set, so I would have to run away to the bush by myself. Being the last day of school for the year, we could leave as soon as the Angelus bell rang and the prayer was said: *The angel of the Lord declared unto Mary and she conceived of the Holy Ghost.*

This was recited by children who still believed in Santa Claus and Humpty Dumpty and repeated without thought to words like "declared unto" and "conceived". I lit candles and said continuous Hail Mary's during the holidays that Sister Chanel would be sent away to teach somewhere else. I even prayed for her to die. She would go to heaven; all nuns went to heaven, so that wouldn't be too bad for her. All my candles went up in smoke, and my prayers must have been snagged in the southerly winds, because there she was on the first day back at school, looking exactly like Hansel and Gretel's wicked stepmother disguised in a nun's habit.

We lined up against the brick wall in our new navy-serge uniforms with black-and-blue ties, felt hat, and new leather ports. And there she was; she hadn't gone to heaven. She hadn't even gone to Woy Woy convent, which was my second choice for her demise.

"Good morning, children. God bless you," she said.

"Good morning, Sister. God bless you," we responded.

"Say it one more time," Sister instructed. "It sounds like you said 'God bless the shoe'. Speak clearly. God is not going to bless my shoe."

One of the boys let out a little giggle, which was cut short by our new teacher's efficient talent of delivering a flick of her fingers to the back of his years, while keeping her rapid stride—seeking her next victim.

"Now, one more time: good morning, children."

"Good morning, Sister. God bless *you*."

Sister nodded her head. "There, *that's* how you will say it. You will march together each morning into the classroom. We will say the morning prayers and then begin our religion lesson, then arithmetic and physical culture, the Angelus prayer, and then lunch. All your school books must be covered with plastic—blue for the girls, the colour of Our Blessed Mother's shawl; and red for the boys, the colour of the bleeding Sacred Heart of Jesus." She continued nodding her head as she spoke. "You have one week to do this, and if your notebooks are not covered by next Monday, you will get the cane. When you sit at your desk, your arms will always be folded unless you are writing. Legs are not to be crossed anywhere, not at the knee or the ankle. You will sit up like good Catholic children, not like heathen Protestants or those barbarians, the children who go to the public school."

Every morning, we lined up against the wall and held out our arms. Our fingers would have to tip the shoulder of the classmate in front of us. We were never to be any closer than arm's distance from the child on each side and to the front. And, Sister said, that should always be a measure of distance between us at all times, not just in school. "And when you get older," she intoned, "keep this distance between you and another person to avoid the occasion of sin."

Our religion lesson began right after the morning prayer. Catechism class usually went beyond the allotted hour, and most times spilled over into our arithmetic lessons, as the former was deemed more important. Faith and religion was the total reason these women had given up so much—or perhaps, so little. The repeated drill of questions and answers from the "Little Green Catechism" went something like this:

Nun: What is man?

Children: Man is one of God's creatures made up by a body and a soul.

Nun: What is hell?

Children (loudly): Hell is a place of eternal torment, made by God to punish those who die in mortal sin.

Nun: What is meant by the unity of God?

Children (spoken not so loudly this time because there was no "hell" word): There is but one God and there can not be more gods than one.

Did we know the meaning of these strange words "blasphemy", "conceived", or "occasion of sin"? They were just big words in our prayers that we had to say, for fear of going to the flames of hell or having the long piece of cane whistle its way through the air down to a small, shaking palm.

Sister Chanel walked around the room, only slapping the idle hands of the children she knew were not at Mass on Sunday. Those children, as well as those who weren't from what she perceived as "good Catholic families", were to sit close to the front of the classroom, as they needed watching every minute. She would peer down at us over her glasses, her lips and nose wrinkled, as if she was looking over an old, dead, smelly wombat left in the sun for days.

Her scrubbed face was red raw, and the tight, starched headdress made it almost impossible for her to turn her head. We soon learned that this didn't stop her from catching us making faces behind her back. She could pivot at a ninety-degree angle faster than a spinning top, before we could get our tongues back in our mouths. With her rimless glasses perched on her pointed nose, she glared and sniffed. "Close your eyes when you pray so you are not thinking about anything else," she instructed.

We had learned from kindergarten and first grade the savvy way of locating nuns in the classroom or coming into the corridor. Actually, it was simple: the big wooden beads they wore looped over a wide black leather belt that would jangle as they walked and became louder as they got closer. But it was not that simple with our dear second class teacher. She had fashioned a way to hold the beads still by twisting them around her left arm, while holding the cane in the other hand. A curious, opened eye while saying prayers would behold her standing right next to the one whose eye was open, and her "I gotcha" look was enough to make Peter O'Malley pee his pants all over the floor and give the rest of us nightmares.

I sat at my wooden desk, feeling underneath it for yesterday's P.K gum. Sister walked up behind me and rapped my fingers with a ruler. The day didn't improve, for true to form as I was a rather clumsy child, and fell over, skinning my knee during what was called "physical culture". The boys were sent to join another class to play cricket. The girls stayed with Sister Chanel on a smaller playground. We were lined up in two rows, face to back, with legs spread apart, as if making a tunnel. The captain of each row bent down and rolled the ball down through the row of open legs. The last girl on the end would pick up the ball and run to the front of the row, bend down, and roll the ball again, until the captain was in front again. The first captain to get to the front was the winner. It seemed strange to me that we could spread our legs for physical culture, bend over and roll a ball under our legs while peeking at our panties, but we couldn't cross our legs in class or wear a short skirt. My clumsy foot lost the game for our team. My knee was bleeding, but Sister Chanel told me to offer the pain up for the souls in purgatory so that they would be let out, and they could run right up to heaven. My pain was their gain.

Rita O'Brien's team won the game, and this pleased Sister, as Rita was a good Catholic girl from a large Catholic family, which made it not a sin that she did impure things with the boys behind the lantana bush. My knee was bleeding, and little pebbles were imbedded in the skin, but if I cried, some poor souls would have to stay in purgatory until there were enough prayers and bleeding knees to get them out. I bit my tongue to stop from crying, but that hurt just as much. Perhaps now the person who was released from purgatory by the bleeding knee could bring a mate out with him because of the additional pain from my biting my tongue.

I became consumed with letting souls out of purgatory and made it a point of throwing myself into a thorny rose bush about once a week, just to release a whole bunch of souls. I could just see them in my head—a group of released souls, waiting for me when I went to heaven and giving me a big party. By the time Auntie Dot went to the local shops for the blue plastic to cover my books, there was none left. I cried and told her I would get the cane if my books weren't covered in blue plastic, and I wasn't sure if that was the kind of pain I could offer up for the holy souls in purgatory. I thought it probably had to be accident pain or deliberate and wilful pain. Never being critical of Catholics, she just shook her head, got on the bus the next day, and went into the city, where she found blue plastic at Woolworth's. Rita O'Brien didn't have the blue plastic on Monday morning, but Sister told her to go over and see Sister Dionysius, as she might have some. Peter and Sandra said there was no blue plastic left at Mr. Barlow's shop—they both screamed before the cane was swiftly lowered to their tiny out stretched palms.

At lunch time I ran down to Sister Helena's class. It smelled of chalk and apples.

"Sister," I said, "why doesn't God answer prayers and candles?"

"Because He is wise and knows what's best for all of us. We must always accept God's will. Say a Hail Mary and try a little harder."

This seemed to be the answer to all trials and tribulations for a certain class. There was still hope, now that I was saying a Hail Mary every day to Our Blessed Mother Mary that Sister Chanel would die—or at least fall down the terrace and break her leg. But I really wanted her dead, so she couldn't put any gum on noses or ribbons in the boys' hair and make them cry. All nuns went to heaven, even if they beat up kids, so praying for her to die, I was sure, was sending her to what she would really want: the eternal joy of being with her God, the Father Almighty, Creator of heaven and earth.

On the days when there was no school, I would be free to dream and make up stories in my head, not to be shared with anyone. I would wait for the first kookaburra's laugh and make up a story about him …

A lone jackass started cackling at the first glimpse of morning light. He tried three times, with four sharp, eager cackles, anxiously trying to motivate an early concert. He was ignored by the rest of his family, who refused to start the frolic before the exact moment of natural decree. Moving down to the end of the branch, he sat and sulked. Minutes later, the sky was teasing with a gradual glimpse of lustrous light. The chorus was now ready and willing, their laughter climbing in unison to a piercing crescendo. The happy soloist conformed and took his place in the choir, with an innate acceptance that the propagation of the species placed limits on his individuality …

Those days, and Australia's birds, were gifts to a child with an imagination.

Many days, our breakfast would be leftover fat from fried bacon slathered on toasted bread. Toast and dripping's, we called it, and it was my favourite. I think of those mornings, so many years ago, every time I am faced with the unpleasant domestic task of getting rid of bacon grease in a fry pan. The present-day vile fat was once something that sustained us during those scarce times. The baker came every day with his horse and cart, selling fresh rolls and bread. The cart had heavy yellow doors on the side and back that, when opened up, would reveal the most delicious smells of warm bread and rolls. I would only hope that the bread man didn't arrive the same time as the dunny man. Without sewers, of course, it was required to have what is referred to in America, in a comparatively refined term, as an "outhouse." we simply called it the "the dunny."

I am sure, however, that somewhere in Australia, the dunny man is still a welcome twice-weekly visitor to the residence. It seems to me that aspiring athletes could take a lesson from this master of the can. Balanced between his shoulder blade and forearm, and with the grace of a ballet dancer lifting a lithe Swan Lake ballerina, the can would be hauled up to the shoulders in a graceful pirouette, without spilling a drop of his clients' shit. A household such as we had, always full of kids and visitors, would never render a half-empty can but one that was always full to the brim. No worries; this great caretaker would leave a fresh can—and sometimes a spare. It was probably a judgement call for the dunny man to leave a spare can, depending on the amount of people he saw hanging around the house. After all, he wouldn't want the can brimming over the next time he came to call. The dunny man, regardless of his individual size, was athletically adept at picking up this full can of faecal matter, which had blended into a soupy, vile liquid with the week's supply of urine. It was always a man—at the time, it was not an equal opportunity employer, so there were no "dunny women"—and he was always whistling and seemed quite happy with his job, despite the fact that the odour seemed to have permeated into his skin. Those who had a dunny man for a friend were always holding their breath in his presence. He may have been scrubbed down with Lysol soap, but the inference of the dunny smell always followed him.

While sitting on the veranda one sunny afternoon, my mother was invited by the Dunny Man to the Dunny Man's Picnic. He told her she was a "good sort", and there would be plenty to eat and drink at this annual event. Stammering and shifting from one foot to the other, he said that he had seen her visiting before and didn't see any husband around. No doubt this brave invitation had been rehearsed in his mind, and he was so nervous and stammering that we feared he'd drop his baggage on the front garden, and this would be more fertilizer than Uncle Pat's pink roses required. In spite of my giggling while listening from the bedroom window, Peggy walked him up the path, smiling with sincere apology. She graciously told him that she was very sorry, but she had to be back in Sydney by the time of the picnic. "But thank you for asking. It sounds like a good time." She put him at ease, and to our relief, his grip on the can became a little steadier. Of course, in the years to come, she would always be teased about her invitation to the Dunny Man's Picnic, especially when she started "bunging on side".

"Oh, yeah," we would say, "you being a good sort really got you far—an invitation to the Dunny Man's Picnic and an offer to be a "rat" in *The Rats of Tobruk*."

It's an Australian thing not to let people get a big head, to bring them down to earth. Bragging about one's self irritates the Aussie psyche.

My mother still took the train up every Friday night. It would chug through Cardiff around 7:00 PM. I would wait for the train to pass under the over-bridge, looking for her wave out of the sooty windows, not caring for the condition of her clothes. I wasn't permitted to go beyond the bridge at such a late hour, but I knew it took exactly ten minutes from the time the train pulled out of the station for her to turn the corner. If I didn't see that beautiful face turn the corner in ten minutes, I waited for twenty. And after twenty, it meant that she had stopped in the pub. It would be getting dark, and I would drag back to the house on the hill to dear Auntie Dot's calm smile.

"Don't worry, luv, she won't be long," she'd tell me.

"I don't care how long she is. I hate the way Apple Blossom perfume smells with the bloody grog."

"Don't swear; it's not ladylike. And be brave. She works so hard."

"When I grow up, I am going to tip all the beer and plonk in the world down the sink."

When finally Peggy did arrive, sometimes well after my bedtime, I would squeeze my eyes shut and pretend to be asleep.

My father filed for divorce, suing on the grounds of desertion. The initial papers were sent by boat mail and took three months to arrive. The sixty-day time allowed to contest or request child support had elapsed, probably when the papers were somewhere on a freighter in the Pacific Ocean. Final divorce decree was sent by efficient air mail and had arrived first, stating no contest or child support had been requested and therefore none would be forthcoming. With no money to spare to hire a lawyer, my mother chalked it up to "that's life". Now she was a divorced woman with a trade. A divorced woman with a trade and a child to support would work next to unmarried men who received higher pay. After my father died many years later, she chose to exalt him in her mind to pre-beatification status, or at least many notches above his deserving scum line.

When I was six years old, Auntie Dot announced on Christmas morning, "Santa Claus was in a hurry and will be back, so here are some plums and nuts and look, a rag doll." It was the strangest rag doll I had ever seen. Stopping for a Christmas drink, and then another, had made "Santa Claus" miss the train from Sydney. Two days later my mother arrived with a doll house, bride doll, and my yearly rubber-lined beach bag, and since that time, I have been suspect of Santa Claus and religious dogmas of faith.

On the first day back to school after the holidays, Sister Chanel asked me to stay after school because she wanted to talk to me. When the last kid had left, she told me to follow her to the playground. We sat under a gum tree in the school yard on a bench. I remember vividly that it was a hot, dry day, and she smelled like medicine and chalk mixed with body odour on her heavy serge garb.

"Why do you come to Mass alone or with Sandra and Peter?" she asked.

"Because they go to the nine o'clock Mass, and we can walk up the hill together," I answered.

"No, I mean, where is your mother and father?"

"I live with Auntie Dot and Uncle Pat."

"Is that your mother's sister?" she inquired.

I shook my head. "No, just a friend."

"What's their name?"

"Poetschka."

She pursed her lips and continued. "Russian. Is Mr. Poetschka from Russia?"

"No, he's from Tamworth."

"Are they Catholic?"

"No, but they make me go to Mass."

"Where are your mother and father?"

"My mother lives in Sydney, and my father is in America."

"Why don't they live together?"

"They're divorced."

"Oh, mercy!" she said closing her eyes and clutching the large crucifix on the end of her rosary beads

"But my mother said that my father might come to Australia and live with us some day, when he gets out of the clink."

"I beg your pardon."

"Yes, Mum said he is in the 'clink' right now, because he sold stuff that he had pinched. Mum said he was always one step ahead of the sheriff, but must have slowed down."

"Oh dear Jesus, Mary, and Joseph! You talk like a gangster, not a young Catholic girl."

The first time that Sister Chanel met my mother was a few weeks later, when we were in the middle of natural science class. Peter had put a small dead goanna in a big jar of grey liquid and was passing it from desk to desk. I looked up from the poor unfortunate goanna and saw my mother, smiling at the doorway. Perhaps out of guilt for missing Christmas, Mum had taken the day off work, got the train from Central to Cardiff, and walked up to the school. Annoyed with the interruption by this woman in a red dress, the devil's colour, with matching lipstick and nail polish, Sister glared,

"Can I help you?"

I was so proud of Mum; she looked like the movie star on the sign at the local pictures, so much more glamorous than the plain aproned mothers who worked in the school tuck shop.

"I thought I would come to meet you, Sister, and I would like to take my daughter for the afternoon."

"She misses a lot of school, but go ahead. Her learning anything is probably a hopeless case anyway."

Two days later, Sister told me that I was going to be put in a good Catholic home. Some orphans would be there, but it was for the best, and I would receive a good Catholic upbringing. I was missing too much school, she informed me, and the truant officer would recommend my placement to the Child Welfare. The parish priest had connections, and he would help get me in. She said I was blessed to be Catholic and that I would be saved from a pagan upbringing. No where in this conversation did she mention my mother or my dear guardians. Apparently the Parish Priest and the Truant officer were the only ones that needed to know. It's true I had been missing school; I faked headaches, vomiting and earaches because I was terrified of Sister Chanel.

I never went back to that school; the next day taking matters into her own hands, auntie Dot marched me over to the local public school. The kids laughed and had fun at the public school; they must not have known that they were going to go to limbo when they died, or they wouldn't have been so cheerful. I don't remember too much about the next few years, probably because they were free from fear and the blessed virtue of humility. I can't remember one bad kid at public school. I learned to play a game called "vigoro", which is similar to cricket, and my clumsy foot seemed to start behaving itself on the short runs to each base. Whenever I saw a nun, especially a sister of Saint Joseph with their familiar heavy starched white round bib, I would run like hell, scared that I would be abducted and placed in a home. Ironically, a few years later, the only one who was put into a home was Sister Chanel, as the poor woman had a nervous breakdown. Her cruelty, however, was only addressed by superiors after a declining enrolment and subsequent loss of money.

The government's solution to the problem of housing shortage in post-war Sydney was to build brick and cement flats, mostly beginning in the inner city suburbs of Redfern and Surry Hills. These flats were havens for the influx of immigrants and war veterans, single mothers, and low-income seniors.

Mr. Jacobsen was the owner of the restaurant where my mother worked a second job in Sydney. She would work in the bindery at the *Sun* newspaper all day and then quickly freshen up to start a shift as a hostess in Mr. Jacobsen's restaurant from 5:30 till 11 PM.

"Peggy, why don't you put yourself on the list for a commission flat?" Mr. Jacobsen asked her one night.

"I don't know, Jake, I think those flats are only for poor buggas."

"Yes, they probably are, Peggy, for poor buggas just like you."

"You get off the *Sun* office an hour early tomorrow, and Mrs. Jacobsen and I will take you down to the office—and you better be there. Don't be like so many of these Australians; they work like dogs and drink it up at the pub, and then if it's not all gone, then off they go to the race track. Get a roof over your head; at least it will give you some security. You can have your daughter live with you and not have to get that late train up to Newcastle every Friday. So you be there in front of the Housing Commission Office at four o clock."

"How many in your family?" the Housing Commission clerk asked.

"Just me and my daughter."

"Where's your husband?"

"In America; he was in the U.S. Navy."

"Those bloody Yanks."

"Oh, no, he's alright; I just didn't like it over there."

"Aw, luv, a good sort like you will be married in no time," he said as he moved her application aside.

Not liking the way this process was evolving, Mr. Jacobsen decided to enter the conversation that he had previously decided should be handled by these two people: his employee and the Housing Commission clerk.

"Look, in case she doesn't get married again, this girl needs a home for herself and her daughter," Mr. Jacobsen interjected. He took note of the clerk's age and the Returned Soldiers League button on his lapel as he continued. "Her father was an ANZAC, came back from France injured, no family home for this girl to come back to. She gets no money from her husband and works two jobs just to survive. Married a man who was in the Battle of Coral Sea, protecting Australia, and what does she get? I tell you, mate, it's bloody awful." ("Mate" was a term that Mr. Jacobsen usually never used, but he thought it would be useful in this case.)

Mum moved into her one-bedroom commission flat in Redfern within two months. It remained the only home she ever wanted for the next thirty-five years. It was close to the pub, shops, and bus and it gave her a cement roof over her head and a door to lock the world out, although it seemed that sometimes the whole world was in that flat.

Arriving on the train that week-end, her face was flush with excitement.

"We have a home now," she announced, "and you can come down to Sydney and live with me, if you want."

As I was about to enter a high school that had the scary words "home science" in its title, moving to Redfern, where there was a milk bar with a juke box at the corner and the Empire picture show right next to that, offered an exciting life for a twelve-year-old. Once more I would try a Catholic school; this time, it would be the same school my mother had attended till the ripe old age of fourteen, when the nuns got her a job in a local printing factory. So I went outside my Redfern parish to my mother's old school, Our Lady of Mount Carmel, Waterloo. Mount Carmel was, and probably still is, run by the Sisters of Mercy. The very term "Sisters of Mercy" made me less apprehensive than an order named after a carpenter. I thought this explained why they were always in arm's length to rulers, sticks, and canes. I used to tell Saint Joseph, whenever I passed his statue in church, with him holding a young Jesus in one arm and a lily in the other, "Do you know what they're doing with those sticks? Not building cupboards, like you were in Jerusalem. They are beating kids, so you better stop it."

But the word "mercy" sounded soft and kind. I said good-bye to my beloved Auntie Dot, Uncle Pat, and Uncle Teddy, and now I would come up to visit them every other week-end.

8

REDFERN HEIGHTS

The small asphalt-paved playground was hot, and the steam rose from its black surface that wrapped around the school and the church. I sat on a bench, waiting to be told where to go after Mum dropped me off on my first day at school, as she hurried to catch her bus to work.

"You'll be alright," she said. "Just ask one of the sisters where to go." And she left.

Three girls about my age whispered together and kept looking over at me and giggling. They were wearing the same uniform as me—black serge tunic, white blouse, blue-and-grey striped tie—but they didn't have the felt hat and gloves. My uniform was brand new; Mum had bought it just the week before.

"Well, luv, we'll be eating tripe and mutton this week," Mum said as she opened her pay packet emptying it out at Grace Bros with two shillings left for a week's school fees.

I wished I looked like these girls did, so fashionable with jingling gold bracelets, their belts tied in a knot, buckle dangling, and their school ties loosened to the point between their breasts. There was nothing I could do to my tunic and blouse to make me look anything other than stupid, as my clothes were always bought two sizes larger, so I could "grow into them". They stood clustered together, giggling, shouting at anyone who dared to come close to the trio, as if plotting a secret plan of untold mayhem. That frightened me; something was going to happen that day, and I feared that something would involve me. I could only make fun of them in my mind, so I secretly called them the Arbuckle's. Fatty Arbuckle was the fat one, who was pretty, with black permed hair; Skinny Arbuckle was the little one, who seemed to always look at Fatty before she did or said anything; and Fanny Arbuckle was my size and height, with brown hair and freckles and a gold tooth.

The smaller children stayed away and if the ball that they were playing with came close to the abominable trio; then it stayed there, unless it was kicked back to the interrupted game nearby. The whispering and giggling stopped when one of the nuns walked out of the convent gate onto the playground, pumping a small hand bell. The ringing got everyone's attention, and they started to line up. They all looked like they knew where they were headed. I didn't.

"Good morning, girls. God bless you."

"Good morning, Sister. God bless you."

Oh, no! I had forgotten about that little ritual. I didn't know where to stand, so to give more time to the situation, I wandered over to the water bubbler.

"You, over there! Where do you think you are going, young lady?"

"To have a drink of water," I replied.

"To have a drink of water, *Sister*," she corrected.

"To have a drink of water, Sister. I am thirsty."

"You should learn to deny yourself. How are you going to stand up against temptation in later life, if you can't deny yourself now?"

I really hadn't thought about denying myself later in life. If I ever day dreamed about my future, it certainly didn't include going without anything, least of all water.

"Who are you anyway?" Sister asked.

"She's a new girl, Sister," offered one of the girls. "She is going to be in our class. Sister told us on Friday that she was coming and that she is from a public school."

"Oh, dear. Well, get in line."

I got in a line where there was a space, and in a second, Sister was over next to me, puffing, with sweat pouring down her face, grabbing my arm with a grip as if I was going to bolt at any time. She shoved me in line next to the Arbuckle's.

"You line up with your class; you will be in Sister Enda's class."

Fatty Arbuckle leaned over to me and whispered, "Sister Enda's a cunt."

One by one, the lines marched off to different classes. I followed the Arbuckle's up the narrow stairway. Halfway up, the blond fat one lagged behind me and grabbed my ankle as I put my other foot on the top stair, and I fell flat on my face. Standing up, I brushed off my uniform and turned around, bolting back down the stairs as fast as I could. I ran down the narrow concrete steps to the outside street, and then I heard the rustle of heavy skirts and the clanking of rosary beads right behind me. It was my new teacher, Sister Mary Enda, behind me in hot pursuit.

"Come on back to class, right this minute!"

I knew if I continued to run, my mother would march me back the next day. The Sisters of Mercy could do no wrong in my mother's eyes. Later, if I ever complained about getting punished or being embarrassed by them, she would always say that I must have deserved it. I realized that I would be deposited back at class the next day, embarrassed and humiliated, in front of the Arbuckle's. I stopped running and turned around, as my new teacher gripped my arm tightly and led me, shuffling, back to the classroom. As we walked back up the stairs, the noise got louder the closer we got to the door. When Sister Enda opened the classroom door, three girls were dancing on top of the desks, pens and books were flying across the room, and the three Arbuckle's were in the corner practicing the "jive".

"Sit down immediately. This is a convent school, not a reformatory." Sister Enda was able to control the class when she was there; she seemed to evoke fear, although I didn't know why. Perhaps it had something to do with her being a "cunt". Whatever Sister Chanel did to me, Sister Enda undid it. I loved her from the first time she chased me down the street. She had white skin with freckles, just like me. She read my compositions to the class, and I could do no wrong in her eyes. Of course, it helped that I started to go to Mass every morning, and said novenas that my mother would stop the drinking and come home after work, and confided my problems to her every week outside the church after benediction. When the music nun caught me finally beating up on the Arbuckle's after six months of torture, Sister Enda said it must have been provoked, and I was not to be punished. I think Sister Enda loved being a nun; she would tell me about the day she entered the convent. When her parents dropped her off at the novitiate and were leaving, she rode to the front gate on the running board of the family car, her last tomboyish act. She told me to say a Hail Mary every day, because no matter what happened to me in life or what I did, I would go to heaven; Our Lady would see to it. She tried to show me how to recognize a true religious vocation, if, for some remote chance, I might have one. And if I didn't enter the convent, she told me, "Keep your eyes wide open before marriage and half-closed after." She made me feel very important and responsible, sending me on errands down to the chemist shop for her favourite brand of soap, Cuticura. She would tell me, "Make sure you are in uniform, and don't forget to tell them it's for the convent as you hand him the shilling." Of course, she knew the shilling would be handed right back, with a grunt and a raised hand.

Sister Enda's efforts to instil a love for Mary could never be shaken. If my intellectual journey of religious doubt through the years was questioned as to whether Jesus was really the son of God and not just a prophet whose subjective tales of miracles were written and translated many years later, Mary would never be included in those misgivings. If nothing more, you had to admire her "chutzpah" for being able to pull off a tale of virgin birth, announced by an angel, and then finding a man to marry her who possessed a trade.

Most of us in the upstairs classroom, the second year of high school, would leave at fourteen years of age and ten months. It was the law, and we took delight in knowing the sisters couldn't do anything about it.

As our fourteen-years-and-ten-months age approached, we would say, one by one, "I am leaving school next week, Sister." Sister Enda would have a look of despair and could be found later that day in the playground, asking the parish priest to intervene and perhaps talk to the parents of the fledgling student, to let her stay at school until she was sixteen. "The character building years", she called them. Most Waterloo and Redfern parents were struggling with many problems of their own and were not given the luxury of indulging their children into a hope of a life beyond working in the factories or, at best, as a clerk typist in an office. Our dreams of perhaps being nurses and teachers were quickly halted by reality, as our paltry pay packets would be needed at home, and to waste two more years on a secondary education was deemed selfish and superior. The Sisters of Mercy at Waterloo were dedicated teachers and knew they had very little time, under the circumstances, to prepare us for whatever we were about to face. Between the required lessons of math, English, and typing, they pounced on vacant time slots to give advice and impart a sense of privilege that we were part of this great universal religion; we were Roman Catholic.

"Some of you don't have a proper home life; we know that. We have visited your homes. Always look into your heart and to your Catholic faith to find what is right. When you fail to do what is right, then look back into your hearts and your religion, and discipline yourself. You will have to be your own conscience."

One of our classes that the Sister at Mount Carmel found absolutely necessary—after religion of course—was elocution. Once a week, a large bosomed lady would come to the school, and try to elevate our speech to one of refinement, thus improving our chances to better ourselves in the years to come.

Instead of saying 'me mother' as we did, we were to say 'my mother'—'sista' was pronounced 'sister' and word pronunciation was dramatized over and over—making us giggle most of the time with adolescent embarrassment, at the repetition of these designed exercises—

Andrew Airway ahh-sked his aunt of her ailment
Billy Boggs dreeeew back the blackboard
Enoch EEEli ate an empty eggshell.

My mother paid and extra shilling for me to take these lessons, over and above the meagre tuition that the nuns charged.

We would plan what would we would do when we were finally free to do just whatever we wanted. My friend Rose said she would come back to the classroom wearing a red dress and low-cut back, burn her uniform, and put ten bob in the class mission box that never seemed to get any more than pennies sent off to the poor, little, black, "fuzzy wuzzy" children in New Guinea. These little cardboard boxes, with a picture of a piccaninny child, were a fixture, right next to the chalk on the shelf below the blackboard. If we had pennies left over after lunch, they would go off to someone in New Guinea, deemed by the Catholic Church as needier than we.

My only ambition was to be a beatnik. I dreamed of spending all my money on beatnik clothes (black stockings, a big sweater that covered my bum); having straight, long hair; and wearing white lipstick. I would hang around coffee shops in Kings Cross and read poetry and look bored. Except the only poetry I knew was "Clancy of the Overflow". Beatniks didn't shake their heads and groove to:

I had written him a letter, which I had for want of better.
Knowledge, sent to where I met him down the Lachlan
years ago.

Rose said to make up my own poetry. Her older sister, Marla, went to the Kings Cross coffee shops, and they just said anything. The real secret was to just look unhappy, don't smile, and "Bob's your uncle".

Mum and I spent those years together sharing one bedroom sleeping in two single beds, a wooden crate in the centre, decorated to resemble a vanity table, with an old mirror and a dark-blue empty bottle of "Evening in Paris" perfume. We would talk back and forth. Every night she would say how lucky we were to have a roof over our head a good job and food and we should thank God. Sometimes we said the rosary together lying in bed. She told me every detail and memory of her "ratbag" American in-laws, softening the tone of her voice when speaking of Mrs. Merry, deaf Lucy, Esther, and Rudy, until finally one of us would fall asleep.

She considered herself an authority on American politics and racial discrimination and would rant, especially after a few drinks, "Everyone criticizes whatever president they have. Poor bloody Eisenhower couldn't even play golf without some bloody mug calling him lazy. Poor bugga, a great general. Gets home from the war, wants to play some golf, the country is at peace—why couldn't he play golf? There will never be another war; we are all safe now. And you would think they won the bloody war single-handed. What about the poor Aussies and the pommies? They were in it for years before the bloody Yanks came in. And the way they treat the poor bloody Negroes—can't even drink in the same water bubbler. But they certainly send them around the world to represent them in the bloody Olympics."

It was 1958, and Wilma Rudolph had won a gold medal in Melbourne. My mother would always have a love/hate relationship with America. But it didn't matter, as her audience would be the women in the pub's ladies lounge or me, and we certainly were not a formidable debating team, nor could we offer another opinion. It was Peggy's identity alone.

Once a year we would receive a wire with one hundred dollars from my father in the U.S. He never sent child support, just one hundred dollars a year—well, most years; the years when he wasn't in jail or the Veterans Hospital for "help". The greeting would read "Merry Christmas. Buy yourself and the kid something". It wasn't enough to change our lives, but for one day we had a good time. Mum could have used it in a million places, but instead, we had a day on the "town". We were rich for a day. We had afternoon tea at the Hotel Australia, with its old dark-red velvet drapes. The cakes and sandwiches, served on a round, silver, three-tiered plate, were wheeled over to us on a cart. Mum knew the head waiter from her time of working nights in the better Sydney restaurants. He would always come over and talk, tell her who was working where, what restaurants were new, and the latest celebrity gossip. Prince Philip was there and had a secret girlfriend with him in one of the suites, he said. And the American crooner Johnny Ray had entertained young men in the hotel, whatever that meant at the time. I didn't know, but I was happy to be part of this grown-up and sophisticated world.

The city's Prince Edward Theatre had an organist playing before the picture and during the interval. The fountain in the lobby added to the regal atmosphere, with its green frog spitting water high into the air. Over the years we saw Green *Dolphin Street*, *The Razor's Edge* and *Showboat*. *Showboat* made Mum cry; she was thinking of Esther and wondering if she ever got to Harlem. After the pictures, we went to Darrell Lea's for chocolate to take home. The bus wasn't good enough for these days on the town; we would take a taxi. "Redfern Heights please, driver," Mum would say, and we would burst into fits of laughter at the joke of elevating Redfern to the "Heights" status that Australian towns want to add after their names, inferring an elite distinction. We would perhaps be able to do this again next year if we received the hundred dollars from my father.

Going to the picture show was the best of times for us; the theatres in Sydney were ornate and offered us a temporary feeling of luxury. Sister Enda was concerned about my going to too many American movies; some of them, she said, were "occasions of sin". We were advised by the Catholic Legion of Decency that if we went to see *God Created Women*, starring Brigitte Bardot, we definitely were committing a mortal sin. I didn't say a word when Mum said she would take me on the next Saturday to see a biblical picture about Adam and Eve and the creation of women. The first scene I remember was Brigitte, naked, behind a sheet. Looking around, I saw only a few men in overcoats but no other females. Mum was the only woman inside the theatre, and I was the only thirteen-year-old. Mum would exclaim "oowa, oowa", as Brigitte bared more of her fabulous body, but we stayed during the entire show, torn between the curiosity and the price of admission.

So the summing up of my sex education was Sister Enda, telling us to keep our eyes closed after marriage; Brigitte Bardot's on-screen naked frolics between two brothers in France; and the used condoms I found scattered around Redfern Park.

The average mean temperature in Sydney is seventy-two degrees; this fact didn't allow too many days that were conducive to wearing a fur coat. But wear it, Mum did. It was a souvenir of her stay in America, Rudy's business finesse, and that at least she had something to show for those years. *Oklahoma* was playing at the State Theatre, and I was to meet her in front of Gowings Department

Store after school. We always met outside of Gowings. Coat styles were changing to shorter, stroller coats, and my mother said it was time to update the coat, take the collar off, and shorten the length. So on an eighty-degree day, before going to see *Oklahoma*, we visited the furrier for a restyling of this precious possession. The furrier was located on Elizabeth Street in the city, with a reputation of quality and expertise—necessary traits for the famous coat from America. When we walked up the stairs and into the store, and there were two-well dressed women engaged in conversation about "mink". One was the customer and the other, obviously the sales lady of the furrier shop. They glanced at us and continued their conversation. We sat on the small couch, watching the two women, and patiently waiting our turn, all the time being ignored. The customer tried on seven coats, pivoting in front of the mirror, admiring herself, and left without buying one. The sales lady turned to us grudgingly, accepting the fact that we wouldn't disappear unless she acknowledged our presence. "Can I help you?"

"I would like to have my coat restyled," Mum said.

She took the coat from my mother as if it were covered in vomit. "What do you want done?"

"I would like the collar off and have it shortened to stroller length. I got in America; my husband bought it for me."

"Yes, I can see that you got it in America from the label, and the design, and of course, the fact that it's cheap."

"Cheap?"

"Yes, cheap. The fur is musk*rat*. I don't know if we will do it."

Embarrassed and dejected, Mum picked up the coat without saying a word.

"It wouldn't be worth your money," the sales lady added. She leaned over the counter and touched the fur again. "Yes, it's definitely musk*rat*."

Mum turned and walked away, eyes erect and flashing, carrying the coat as if it were a sacred garment. "*Rat?* Must have been a bloody big rat to make a coat out of it," she mumbled on the way down the stairs, with me hanging onto the other arm. She didn't laugh during *Oklahoma,* just smiled when her favourite character in the movie sang, *"I'm just a girl who can't say no* ..." And later, I saw tears run down those beautiful high cheek bones. I wasn't sure if it was for the sad part of the movie or the realization that she would probably never feel the pride again in wearing her coat; it wouldn't be the same, changed in two minutes by an unthoughtful, snobbish sales lady. It was her only souvenir of her marriage, a gift from an uncaring man who, for a brief moment in his marriage, perhaps out of guilt, wanted to grant a wish to this woman he had left alone every night, thousands of miles from her beloved home.

My mother had to pass five pubs between the *Sun* office and our flat in Redfern on her way home from work. The seduction of the activity on a hot afternoon, after working in a factory all day, proved tempting to a woman in her thirties. The Ladies Lounge gave respectability to a woman who was "just stopping in for one". And the thrill of a man, glancing through the bar, making eye contact with the ladies, filled the flirtation desire that was missing from her single life. The pubs closed at six o'clock, and I would watch the clock and know that she would be home soon. Husbands and sons went home to long-suffering wives and longer-suffering mothers. I would hang out the window, looking up the street, and glance at the mantle clock that sat on the sideboard. At around ten minutes after six, she would come into view, her short, wavy auburn hair parted on the side. She looked up at the window and waved. If she didn't wave and smile at me as I hung out of the third-floor window, I would feel a dread from my throat to my feet. I had learned, within a short few months that nothing I did could avoid the insults or the feeling of unspoken resentment of my very presence and its burden of responsibility that her drinking brought to the surface. My adoration of this beautiful woman, who was my mother and my only family, turned into fear some time between my thirteenth and fourteenth birthdays. The laughter would be less, with further intervals. Alcohol is a clever stalker, choosing those who bask in its early stages of uninhibited calm. It's not a coincidence that women are prone to alcoholism. It's not a pre-disposed gene. My mother was stuck in a time when she was subject to the collective opinion of a society that exalted the "housewife" and blamed the failure of divorce on, if nothing else, using poor judgement—even if those decisions were made during a time of war, when life seemed so fragile, and there was urgency to soak up every euphoric pleasure before the opportunity could end forever. Disguising itself as a friend, stroking her needs, alcohol imbedded its unshakable claws into her soul.

After much debate and a vote, the pubs were allowed to stay open till 9:00 PM. While some saw this as social progress, it was seen by many as fuelling the fire for the segment of the Australian population that stopped by for a "quickie" on their way home from work. Wives and children were silent enablers, bracing to accept their lot of abuse, both physical and verbal, only now it would be later in the evening. It was an acceptance that would affect the rest of their lives. If they found the strength and did not become alcoholics themselves, they might subconsciously chose dependant partners or to be the care-giver of the weak. The process from social drinking to problem drinking is selective, as to who will be its victims. It is a selection that knows no barriers of class, money, education, or race. All have a common need to escape to a warm feeling of supreme confidence, blinded to its artificial offering.

Pay nights were Friday, and after stopping in the Ladies Parlour at the Norfolk pub, Peggy would lay out the week's groceries. Out of the string bag would come a leg of mutton, two pork chops, and a bar of Sunlight soap, which could be used to wash hair, dishes, clothes, and even floors? The other bag would contain a bottle of Penfolds Cream Sherry.

"Mum, why do you buy that plonk?" I would ask.

"It's not plonk; it's sherry," she'd respond, putting on her best imitation of dignified speech, with raised eyebrows and nose in the air. "And it's for medicinal purposes. And furthermore, young lady, it's really none of your business."

> *Dear Mother of God, tell your son to change all the plonk in the world to water. Like He did at the marriage feast of Cana, but the other way around. Please, please, dear Lady. Sister Enda says He can't turn you down for any favour.*

After a few drinks on those days, I lost the beautiful, smiling, funny woman who was my unorthodox mother. For a brief time on Saturday morning, we sat in the little kitchen, looking over the vacant lot that soon would be filled with more multi-story brick housing commission flats. Till that time, our third-floor one-bedroom flat had an uninterrupted view of Redfern Park from the kitchen window, on those fresh, sunny, Australian mornings with an early promise of the scorching hot day to come. The winking pigeons, with their red-brown eyes, perched on the window sill every morning, waiting for bread crumbs; they were my only pets. The park bustled on a Saturday afternoon, busy getting ready for South Sydney's Rabbits football games—the "The Rabbo's" with the familiar green-and-red jerseys.

I would read everything I could. The racy Sydney newspapers always had a girl in a bathing suit on the cover. I never did understand why that would be on the front cover of a newspaper. Working at the *Sun*, which at that time had changed to the *Sun Herald*, my mother would bring home *Look* magazine and *Women's Day*.

For me, at that time, Sydney was about the best place to live, as I could be amused for hours and would walk from Redfern through Surry Hills and on to the city. Wandering around the city offered me escape into my own world—a tree or bench in the botanical gardens; watching the ferries lumber back and forth across the glistening harbour suburbs; silent prayers in St. Mary's Cathedral; throwing pennies into the Archibald Fountain in Hyde Park; window shopping in the arcades; the fabulous Mitchell Library, which always seemed open to give me a haven. I loved the vibrant pulse of Dixon Street in the heart of Chinatown; seemingly more authentically Chinese in the 1950s, with its backyard cages of birds and hanging, skinned ducks. The library offered me newspapers from all over the world, and I could spend hours peacefully reading, safe and without argument, and soon I erroneously fancied myself as well informed on current and historical events. The problem was that there was no one to really debate. I tried with Sister Enda, but she always brought the conversation back to being a good Catholic girl, and all bad things that happen to us should be offered up for the souls in purgatory and accepting God's will.

"Mum, do you know that Australia only allows white people to move here?" I once asked her.

"What do you mean?"

"Well, you are always talking about the treatment of Negroes in America, but Australia doesn't let any Negroes live here."

"Don't be silly. What do you think Aborigines are?"

"Well, they were here first, but Australia doesn't let any American Negroes in the country. If your friend Esther wanted to move here, she couldn't."

Taking advantage of the silence, thinking her wrinkled brow meant she was contemplating what I was saying, I persisted, mistakenly believing that this would lead to an enjoyable debate of critical thinking and weighing both sides. "And furthermore, did you know that there were a lot of Jews killed, and the Pope did nothing about it, and Hitler was an altar boy?"

"Don't you ever say anything about the Pope!" she said angrily. "You will go to hell! You better ask God's forgiveness." The conversation abruptly ended when she threw a plate hitting my head. The next morning, I found her asleep on the kitchen floor. I helped her to bed, cleaned up the kitchen, and took the empty bottles of whiskey and cream sherry. It was Sunday; I went to Mass with an empty bottle in one hand and a Catholic missal in the other. I dropped the bottle in the garbage can behind the flats. I didn't ask God's forgiveness for my criticism of the Pope; I just prayed for my mother to stop drinking and I never would display my pseudo-intellect again. I became adept at side-stepping subjects that would annoy her, especially after the second drink, which might trigger her frustration and misplaced anger. Our conversations would be simple and superficial, relevant to the moment and problems at hand. My very presence, when she was drinking, seemed to ignite a resentment that defied who she was and the love I knew she had for me. There were many more times when she was caring and loving and took pride in my smallest accomplishments, and those are the memories I choose to remember and cherish.

My mother died in 1982 at age sixty-one. I was living in the U.S. and flew to Sydney for a month when she was diagnosed with cancer. Accompanied by one of my oldest friends from the Mount Carmel days, we searched for a nursing home in the Sydney suburbs. Some were beautiful properties, with caring and patient proprietors, one overlooking one of Sydney many lovely beaches. I knew this would not make her happy; aesthetics had never been important to her, and she was content when an opening came with the Sydney City Mission Home in Redfern. The kind people there turned her bed around so she could look in the direction of her beloved one-bedroom Redfern flat.

The doctors said she had about five months to live. Father Doyle from Mount Carmel, who came to give her the last rites, told me she had six weeks. I returned home to the U.S., my family, and my job, and planned on going back in three months. She died six weeks later to the day that Father Doyle had predicted. As in the past, her good friend Gladys was there by her side, and both she and her family took care of all the final arrangements, as they had for her mother so many years before.

On one of my last trips to Sydney, I walked from Redfern Station down to Walker Street. The commission flats hadn't seen the rapid decay that the American projects have seen. It had been almost fifty years since the day we moved into the only home my mother ever wanted. I walked around to see if the gas box was still there, the one I had sat on so many times, waiting for her to cross through the yard on her way home from work. The old copper boiler, where we would boil and scrub our clothes weekly, was no longer in the laundry rooms. I must have looked suspicious, poking around, as a young man asked me if I was a social worker looking for an address. I told him I wasn't, that I used to live in that flat. I pointed to the one on the end of the three-story brick building, now dwarfed by other, much taller brick buildings. We spent time talking about the area. I told him how it had been many years ago, when the view from the window allowed a full vision of Redfern Park, how it buzzed with activity on Saturday afternoons, and how the police paddy wagons always surrounded the park on Soccer Days, anticipating the inevitable fighting among the fans. He told me he was from Iraq and loved Australia, but he missed his home and his mother. His English was good, and he seemed well educated and a gentleman. America had already invaded Iraq by that time and seemed to be stuck in a mission that had no end in sight. We had just learned of the treatment of the Iraqi prisoners by American soldiers at Abu Ghraib—actions that contradicted everything America stands for—

> *If we ever pass out as a great nation, we ought to put on our tombstone, "America died from a delusion that she has moral leadership."*
>
> Will Rogers, 1880–1935

I thought of my grandfather and his old mate Mick, sitting in the backyard many years before, not too far down the street from where I was standing. They would talk to each other, as only old soldiers can, questioning the fertility of their mission in the war that would "end all wars".

We are mostly unwitting participants in religion, politics, and wars that affect our lives. We have to continue the battle to erase the filthy language of racial prejudice, heard and accepted as every day conversation by past and present generations. Our parents usually choose our religion, but politics and wars are determined by where we just happen to live—poverty mostly by the accident of birth. My mother, who was at a Sydney nightclub, met an American sailor, and her life was forever defined in those brief minutes. Young men and women sign up at a recruiting office to see the world and later are returned home in coffins.

History confirms that great nations and super-powers pass out at about three hundred years. Perhaps Will Rogers's prediction of the possibility of the United States "passing out" might be inevitable, unable to reverse the edicts of history.

But the soul of the United States and its historic determination to put things right, should never to be under estimated. Presently, war-weary Americans are voting for change in record numbers. They are sleeping giants when put to task, and in the spirit of their forefathers, they are refusing to pass out and let their morals die. If ever the factual doomed lessons of history battle the will of the American people, my money is "ON THE BLOODY YANKS."

GLOSSARY OF AUSTRALIAN SLANG

ANZAC:	Members of the Australian and New Zealand Army Corps in World War 1. Presently, any soldier of Australia and New Zealand.
Battler:	handles life struggles with courage.
Bludger:	a person who relies on someone else for his support, or who gains from the work of others.
Bugger (taboo slang):	an unpleasant or difficult person; is used sometimes for a person down on their luck (e.g.: "poor bugga")
Bung on side:	acting snobbish.
Digger:	Australian or New Zealand Soldier.
Dunny:	outside toilet.
Mug (slang):	a person who is easily swindled or is stupid.
Loo:	toilet.
Play up:	cause trouble.
Plonk:	cheap inferior wine.
Pommy:	person from Britain
Poofter:	an offensive term for a homosexual man; is used also as a general Term for a man with unlikeable traits.
Ratbag:	a person who is an offbeat trouble-maker
Sticky beak:	a nosy, interfering person
Tooheys:	a brand of beer
Wattle and waratah:	native Australian plants
Whinge:	complain
Yank:	term for all Americans, not just Northerners, when used outside the U.S.

Credits

Wortman, Art, *Selected Collection, Will Rogers Wise & Witty Sayings,* (Hallmark Editions, 1969), 13, 14,136.

Farnsworth, Clyde H, "Burnum Burnum—Fighter for Australia's Aborigines" *New York Times*, August 20, 1997, Obituaries, 96, 97.

Martin, Elaine, "Social Work and Women's Equality in Post War Australia", *Women's History Review 2003* (Flinders University, Adelaide Australia), 99-100

On its Web site, Australian Gov. Immigration Fact Sheet. http://www.immi.gov.au/facts/08abolition.html. 103-104,

Made in United States
North Haven, CT
17 August 2023

40403275R00086